Get Started In Thai

David Smyth

First published in Great Britain in 2015 by Hodder and Stoughton.
An Hachette UK company.

Copyright © David Smyth 2015

The right of David Smyth to be identified as the Author of the Work has been asserted by him in accordance with the Copyright, Designs and Patents Act 1988.

Database right Hodder & Stoughton (makers)

The *Teach Yourself* name is a registered trademark of Hachette UK.

British Library Cataloguing in Publication Data: a catalogue record for this title is available from the British Library.

Library of Congress Catalog Card Number: on file.

ISBN: 9781444798777

1

The publisher has used its best endeavours to ensure that any website addresses referred to in this book are correct and active at the time of going to press. However, the publisher and the author have no responsibility for the websites and can make no guarantee that a site will remain live or that the content will remain relevant, decent or appropriate.

The publisher has made every effort to mark as such all words which it believes to be trademarks. The publisher should also like to make it clear that the presence of a word in the book, whether marked or unmarked, in no way affects its legal status as a trademark.

Every reasonable effort has been made by the publisher to trace the copyright holders of material in this book. Any errors or omissions should be notified in writing to the publisher, who will endeavour to rectify the situation for any reprints and future editions.

Cover image © Shutterstock.com.

Typeset by Graphicraft Limited, Hong Kong.

Printed and bound in Great Britain by CPI Group (UK) Ltd., Croydon CR0 4YY.

John Murray Learning policy is to use papers that are natural, renewable and recyclable products and made from wood grown in sustainable forests. The logging and manufacturing processes are expected to conform to the environmental regulations of the country of origin.

John Murray Learning
Carmelite House
50 Victoria Embankment
EC4Y 0DZ
www.hodder.co.uk

Also available
as an ebook

Contents

Acknowledgements

I am indebted to Sujinda Khantayalongkoch for checking the Thai script and sharing her insights on the language. I am also extremely grateful to Alison Macaulay for her sympathetic and meticulous editing of the manuscript. Errors, omissions and other shortcomings are, however, entirely my own responsibility.

About the author

David Smyth recently retired as Senior Lecturer in Thai at SOAS, University of London after teaching Thai at different levels there for more than 30 years. He is the author of *Teach Yourself Complete Thai* and *Thai: An Essential Grammar*, and has translated a number of Thai novels and short stories into English.

How this book works

Welcome to *Get Started in Thai*! This course is designed for complete beginners. It will provide you with the basic vocabulary and grammar to cope with a number of common situations which you are likely to be faced with in Thailand. It also teaches you, step-by-step, how to read Thai script. If you don't want to spend the time learning how to read and write Thai, you can ignore those sections of each unit and simply work through the book in Romanized Thai. But if you do so, you won't be getting your money's worth from the course and you'll be severely limiting your prospects for making progress in the language beyond a very elementary level. Learn how to read, however, and you will find that traffic signs, advertisement hoardings, menus, shop signs and magazines suddenly spring to life and help you to improve your vocabulary and understanding of the grammar; you will find your pronunciation improves, too, because you are no longer trying to think of Thai sounds in terms of the Latin alphabet; you will find that Thais can help you more easily; and you will find that by becoming literate in Thai, you can take control of your own learning, by finding things to read that interest you personally.

Now that you have been persuaded that you really do want to learn to read Thai, there is some good news. The Thai script is presented here in such a way as to show you that it is neither extremely difficult nor time consuming and that even if you are one of the least gifted language learners, you can, with regular practice, learn to read and write Thai. What is needed is the patience and persistence to copy out letters, words and then phrases a sufficient number of times until they become almost second nature. Keep going back over earlier lessons, because by reading material that is familiar, you will begin to read more quickly and develop the ability to recognize words instantly without having to labour over individual letters each time. Eventually, copying out whole conversations will improve not only your reading and writing skills but will also reinforce everything else you have learned about the language, including pronunciation and grammar.

Each unit in *Get Started in Thai* is structured in the following way:

What you will learn identifies what you will be able to do in Thai by the end of the unit.

Culture point presents an interesting cultural aspect related to the unit theme, introduces some key words and phrases and includes a challenging question for you.

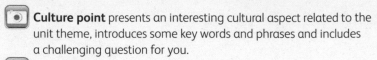 **Vocabulary builder** introduces key unit vocabulary grouped by theme and conversations, and is accompanied by audio.

Conversations are recorded dialogues you can listen to and practise, beginning with a narrative that helps you understand what you will hear, a focusing question and follow-up activities.

Language discovery draws your attention to key language points in the conversations, whether it is a grammar rule or a way of saying things. Read the notes and look at the conversations to see how the language is used in practice and to reinforce your understanding of the language.

Practice offers a variety of exercises to give you a chance to 'pull it all together' and make active use of the language.

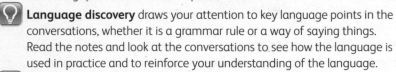 **Speaking and listening** offers copious practice in speaking and understanding Thai through exercises that let you use what you have learned in the unit and previously. Try to do the speaking activity spontaneously. The listening activities increase your understanding of spoken Thai.

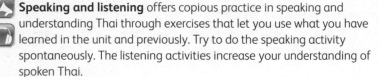 **Reading and writing** provides a carefully graded introduction to the Thai system of writing, introducing a few letters at a time and explaining clearly how the tone rules operate. The examples in each unit are presented in Thai script with Romanization below; cover up the Romanization to test how well you can read the Thai, and then listen to the audio and follow the words in the book in Thai script.

Test yourself helps you assess what you have learned. Do the tests without looking at the text.

Self-check lets you see what you can do in Thai after mastering each unit. When you feel confident that you can use the language correctly, move on to the next unit.

You will also find **Review** units, and appendices providing an **Answer key**, a **Thai–English glossary**, a list of **Thai numbers** and the **Thai alphabet**.

Study the units at your own pace, and remember to make frequent and repeated use of the audio.

To help you through the course, a system of icons indicates the actions you should take:

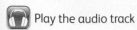 Play the audio track

 Culture tip

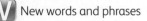 New words and phrases

 Listen and pronounce

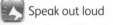 Figure something out for yourself

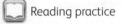 Speak out loud

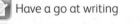 Exercises coming up

Reading practice

Have a go at writing

Check your Thai ability (no cheating!)

As you work your way through the course, you will also become familiar with studying on your own, looking things up and checking your Thai language ability.

Here are some resources you can always consult:

Pronunciation guide provides an overview of Thai and tones sounds. We encourage you to practise pronunciation as you begin the course and go over it regularly. You can find the guide at the beginning of the book.

Review units allow you to consolidate what you have learned in previous units. You can judge from your answers whether you are ready to move on, or whether you need to go back and refresh or consolidate what you have been learning.

Answer key helps you to monitor your performance and check your progress.

Thai–English glossary allows you to quickly access the vocabulary that is presented in the course.

Thai alphabet appendix provides a full list of consonants and vowels and their Romanized equivalents.

Thai numbers appendix shows how numbers are formed in Thai.

Learn to learn

The Discovery method

There are lots of approaches to language learning, some practical, some quite unconventional. Perhaps you know of a few, or even have some techniques of your own. In this book we have incorporated the **Discovery method** of learning, a sort of DIY approach to language learning. What this means is that you will be encouraged throughout the course to engage your mind and figure out the language for yourself, through identifying patterns, understanding grammar concepts, and so on. This method promotes language awareness, a critical skill in acquiring a new language. As a result of your own efforts, you will be able to better retain what you have learned, use it with confidence, and, even better, apply those same skills to continuing to learn the language (or, indeed, another one) on your own after you've finished this book.

Everyone can succeed in learning a language – the key is to know how to learn it. Learning is more than just reading or memorizing grammar and vocabulary. It's about being an active learner, learning in real contexts, and, most importantly, using what you've learned in different situations. Simply put, if you figure something out for yourself, you're more likely to understand it. And when you use what you've learned, you're more likely to remember it.

And because many of the essential grammar rules are introduced through the **Discovery method**, you'll have fun while learning. Soon, the language will start to make sense and you'll be relying on your own intuition to construct original sentences independently, not just listening and repeating.

Enjoy yourself!

Tips for success

1 MAKE A HABIT OUT OF LEARNING

Study a little every day, between 20 and 30 minutes if possible, rather than two to three hours in one session. Give yourself short-term goals, e.g. work out how long you'll spend on a particular unit and work within the time limit. This will help you to create a disciplined routine, in the same way you would if you were training for a sport or practising a musical instrument. You will need to concentrate, so try to create an environment conducive to learning which is calm and quiet and free from distractions. As you study, do not worry about your mistakes or the things you can't remember or understand. Languages settle differently in our brains, but gradually the language will become clearer as your brain starts to make new connections. Just give yourself enough time and you will succeed.

2 EXPAND YOUR CONTACT WITH THE LANGUAGE

Make use of the internet to access sites where you can listen to – and see – Thais speaking. Songs, films, news items and Thai language-learning materials can nowadays be accessed very easily.

3 VOCABULARY

▶ Organize your study of vocabulary. Group new words under **generic categories** such as *family members* or *food*; **situations** in which they occur such as *shopping* or *asking for directions*; and **functions** such as *apologizing* or *asking for help with your Thai*.

▶ Write the words over and over. Keep lists on your smartphone or tablet, or in a notebook.

▶ Listen to the audio several times and say the words out loud as you hear or read them.

▶ Cover up the English translations and try to remember the meanings.

▶ Create flash cards, drawings and mind maps.

4 GRAMMAR

▶ Keep a record of grammatical rules with examples and add further examples and new information as you go along. This will help you to increase your awareness of the structure of the language and enable you to process new information more efficiently.

▶ Think about how the rules of Thai compare with your own language or other languages you may speak.

5 PRONUNCIATION

▶ Keep a section of your notebook for sounds and words that give you trouble. Practise them separately.

▶ Repeat all of the conversations, line by line, trying to mimic the intonation of the speakers.

▶ Record yourself and compare yourself to a native speaker.

▶ Learning short phrases rather than single words is an effective way of not only improving pronunciation, but also memorizing vocabulary and internalizing grammatical rules.

6 LISTENING AND READING

▶ **Imagine the situation.** Try to imagine the scenes and make educated guesses about the topic and vocabulary.

▶ **Get the gist.** Concentrate on the main part and don't worry about individual words.

▶ **Guess the meaning of key words.** Use the context and your own experience or knowledge of the topic to guess the sorts of words in a reading passage or dialogue.

▶ **Re-read, re-read, re-read!** When learning a new script, improve your confidence and fluency by frequently reviewing old familiar material. Musicians don't deliver their best performance when sight-reading a piece of music for the first time, nor do beginning language learners read unfamiliar material fluently in a strange script. Spend a lot of time working on the familiar and gradually your ability to deal with the new and unfamiliar will improve.

▶ **Copy, copy, copy!** Copying out words, phrases and conversations will greatly improve the speed at which you learn to read Thai script, not to mention your handwriting. At the same time it will help you to remember vocabulary and grammatical patterns, and even improve your pronunciation.

7 SPEAKING

Rehearse in the foreign language. Successful learners overcome their inhibitions and get into situations where they must listen to and speak the foreign language. Here are some tips:

▶ Speak out loud as you go through the course. Speak along with the characters in the conversations and then practise taking a part in the dialogues. Think how you might customize their responses to suit you.

► Translate the world around you. Look at objects around you and try to name them in Thai; and try to translate everyday transactions such as shopping, ordering food, asking directions and introducing yourself, into Thai.

► Try to find sympathetic native speakers with whom you can practise.

8 LEARN FROM YOUR ERRORS

► Don't let errors interfere with getting your message across. Mistakes are a normal part of any learning process.

► Realize that many errors are not serious. Making a mistake in the tone of a word, for example, does not necessarily mean that your listener will not understand what you have said. The context will provide clues and many Thais are sympathetic listeners when foreigners are trying to speak their language.

9 LEARN TO COPE WITH UNCERTAINTY

► **Don't panic if you don't understand.** Just keep going and try to guess what is being said or, if you cannot, isolate the expression or words you haven't understood and have them explained to you.

► **Keep talking.** The best way to improve your fluency in a foreign language is to speak it. Try to talk at every opportunity to do so. Prepare questions in advance – and anticipate likely responses – so that you can control the direction of the conversation and keep it flowing. Don't worry about mistakes; and if you get stuck for a particular word, use the English word.

► **Don't over-use a dictionary.** Don't be tempted to immediately look up every word you don't know. Underline new ones and read the conversation several times, concentrating on trying to get the gist of the passage. If after the third time there are still words which prevent you from getting the general meaning of the passage, look them up in the glossary or a suitable dictionary.

The Thai language

Thai is the national language of Thailand and is spoken by approximately 60 million people in that country. Lao, spoken in neighbouring Laos, is very closely related to Thai (although most Thais from Bangkok would have some difficulty understanding it), but the other neighbouring languages – Burmese, Cambodian and Malay – are completely different. Distinct dialects of Thai are spoken in the north, northeast and south of the country, but it is the language of the Central Region and Bangkok which is used throughout the country as the medium for education and mass media and which is taught in this course.

Thai is a tonal language. In tonal languages the meaning of a syllable is determined by the pitch at which it is pronounced. **kao:**, for example, means *news* when pronounced with a low tone, *white* with a rising tone and *rice* with a falling tone. If tones make pronunciation in Thai seem more complex than in more familiar European languages, you will probably find Thai grammar considerably easier to absorb, for there are no complex verb tenses and noun endings which seem to blight many people's experience of trying to learn a foreign language.

Thai is written in its own unique alphabetic script which has developed from a script originally found in India. It is written across the page from left to right, with certain vowels appearing above the line of writing and others appearing below. There are no spaces between words; when spaces do occur, they act as a form of punctuation mark, similar to commas and full stops.

Romanization of Thai

For Westerners learning the language it is convenient to use Romanized Thai at the beginning, but it must be stressed that this is no more than a learning aid. It is not an acceptable alternative to the Thai script and most Thais would not be able to read Thai written in Romanized form. There are a number of different systems of Romanizing Thai, each with its advantages and disadvantages. Like all systems, the one used in this book can offer only an approximate representation of the Thai sound. The most effective strategy is to learn pronunciations from the audio and to memorize Thai script spellings rather than Romanized spellings. You should think of the Romanization system as a crutch and aim to discard it as quickly as possible.

Pronunciation guide

There are a few sounds in Thai that do not exist in English and which can cause some problems. But the vast majority of Thai sounds have a reasonably close equivalent in English.

Consonants

 00.01

At the beginning of a word, consonants are generally pronounced as in English. A few sounds, however, need further clarification:

g as in *get* (not *gin*)

ng a single sound which we are familiar with in English at the end of words like *wrong* and *song*, but which also occurs at the beginning of words in Thai:

ngahn   ngâi: ngahm   ngoo

bp a single sound which is somewhere between a *b* sound and a *p* sound in English. Many learners find it hard to both produce this sound accurately and to distinguish it from **b**. Don't be discouraged if you do have problems; you will probably find that over a period of time you will gradually master it:

bpai   bpen   bpoo   bplào

dt a single sound which is somewhere between a *d* sound and a *t* sound in English. Again, many learners find it difficult to distinguish from **t** at first, although usually such problems are short-lived:

dtàir   dtìt   dtorn   dtrong

At the end of a word the sounds **k**, **p** and **t** are not 'released'. Examples of 'unreleased' final consonants in English include the *t* in *rat* when *rat trap* is said quickly and the *p* in the casual pronunciation of *yep!* At first you may feel that words ending in **k**, **p** and **t** all sound the same, but within a very short time you will find that you can hear a distinct difference:

bpàhk   bàhp   bàht

yâhk   yàhp   yâht

Many Thais have difficulty pronouncing an **r** sound and will substitute a **l** sound instead. Thus, **a-rai?** (*what?*) becomes **a-lai?** In words that begin with two consonants, you might also hear some Thais omit the second consonant sound. **krai?** (*who?*) becomes **kai?** and **bplah** (*fish*) becomes **bpah**.

Vowels

 00.02

Most Thai vowels have near equivalents in English. In the romanization system used in this book, vowels are pronounced as follows:

a	as in *ago*
e	as in *pen*
i	as in *bit*
o	as in *cot*
u	as in *fun*
ah	as in *father*
ai, ai:	as in *Thai*
air	as in *fair*
ao, ao:	as in *Lao*
ay	as in *may*
ee	as in *fee*
er	as in *number*
ew	as in *few*
oh	as in *go*
OO	as in *book*
oo	as in *food*
oy	as in *boy*

Other sounds, however, have no near equivalent in English and you need to listen to the audio to have a proper idea of how they should be pronounced:

eu:	**meu:**	**séu:**	**keu:**
eu-a	**mêu-a**	**sêu-a**	**nĕu-a**
air-o	**láir-o**	**gâir-o**	**tăir-o**
er-ee	**ler-ee**	**ker-ee**	**ner-ee**

Tones

 00.03

There are five tones in Thai: mid tone, low tone, high tone, rising tone and falling tone. These are represented in the romanization system by the following accents: mid tone (no mark), low tone (ˋ), high tone (ˊ), rising tone (ˇ) and falling tone (ˆ). To help you attune your ears to the different tone sounds, listen to the audio of a Thai speaker saying the following words. Don't worry about the meanings at this stage – simply concentrate on listening:

mid tone	kOOn	krai	mah	bpai
	pairng	mee	dairng	bpen
low tone	jàhk	bpàirt	sìp	bàht
	yài	jòrt	èek	nèung
high tone	mái	káo	lót	lék
	róo	rót	náhm	púk
rising tone	sǒo-ay	pǒm	sǒrng	kǒr
	sěe-a	kǒrng	nǎi	děe-o
falling tone	mâi	châi	dâi	têe
	gâo:	mâhk	chôrp	pôot

It is obviously important to be able both to hear and to reproduce tones correctly if you are going to make yourself understood. But don't let a fear of getting a tone wrong inhibit you. Surprisingly, wrong tones are very seldom the cause of misunderstandings and communication breakdowns. Indeed, many non-Thais operate confidently and effectively in the language with far from perfect accuracy in their tones.

1 sa-wùt dee, bpai lá ná, kòrp-kOOn, kǒr-tôht

Hello, goodbye, thank you, sorry

In this unit you will learn how to:
▶ *say* hello *and* goodbye.
▶ *use polite particles and basic courtesy phrases, such as* thank you, sorry *and* never mind.
▶ *address people appropriately.*
▶ *recognize the most common low class consonants and read some simple words.*

CEFR: *(A1) Can establish basic social contact by using the simplest everyday polite forms of greetings and farewells; can say* thank you *and respond to thanks; can say* sorry *and respond to apologies.*

Names and greetings

Thais use first names, not family names in most situations. When addressing or referring to a Thai by name, whether male or female, you should normally use the polite title **kOOn** (usually spelt **Khun** in Romanized Thai, and roughly equivalent to *Mr, Mrs, Miss, Ms*) in front of their name. You can do this even when you are speaking English, as a sign of politeness. In Thai, if you omit **kOOn**, it indicates that you think the other person is either a very close friend, a child, or of markedly inferior social status. So, best to play safe!

Personal names – like place names – are not always pronounced as you might guess from the Romanized spelling. For example **Chatichai** is pronounced **Châht-chai:** (not 'chat-ee-chai'), **Vantana** is pronounced **Wun-ta-nah** (not 'van-tan-a') and **Phornthip** is pronounced **Porn-típ** (not 'forn-thip'). Thais are usually far too polite to correct your mispronunciation, so it is a good idea – and a sign of simple respect – to check from the beginning that you can pronounce their name correctly.

The greeting/farewell, **sa-wùt dee**, can be used at any time of the day and is often accompanied by a **wai**, a gesture in which the head is bowed slightly and the hands held in a prayer-like position, somewhere between the neck and forehead.

 Which Thai word should you use in front of someone's name so as not to sound overly familiar or informal?

Language discovery 1

POLITE PARTICLES

Before we learn even the simplest expressions, we need to know the polite particles, **krúp**, used by males, and **kà** (low tone, short vowel) or **kâh** (falling tone, long vowel) – the choice is yours – used by females. Polite particles are untranslateable words added at the end of a sentence to indicate – you guessed it – that the speaker is being polite.

Vocabulary builder

01.01 **Listen to the audio, and try to imitate the speakers as closely as you can.**

NAMES AND TITLES

ครับ	krúp	*male polite particle*
ค่ะ; คะ	kà/kâh; ká	*female polite particles*
ผม	pŏm	*I (male speaker)*
ฉัน	chún	*I (female speaker)*
ไป	bpai	*to go*
คุณ	kOOn	*polite title: Mr/Mrs/Miss/Ms*
อาจารย์	ah-jahn	*teacher, lecturer*
มาก	mâhk	*very, much*

NEW EXPRESSIONS

สวัสดี	sa-wùt dee	*hello; good morning/afternoon/ evening; goodbye*
ไปละนะ	bpai lá ná	*goodbye (informal)*
ขอบคุณมาก	kòrp-kOOn mâhk	*thank you very much*
ขอโทษ	kŏr-tôht	*I'm sorry; excuse me*
ไม่เป็นไร	mâi bpen rai	*you're welcome; never mind; it doesn't matter*

Conversation 1: *Hello* and *goodbye*

 01.02 *Steve is greeting a Thai friend.*

1 What is the friend's name?

Steve	สวัสดีครับคุณวันเพ็น	sa-wùt dee krúp kOOn Wun-pen
Friend	สวัสดีค่ะคุณสตีฟ	sa-wùt dee kà kOOn Sa-dteef

2 Read and listen to the conversation again.

Listen carefully to how Steve's friend's name is pronounced. Although it is normally written **Wanpen**, the first syllable **Wan** rhymes with *run*, not *ran*. Notice, too, how Steve's name is pronounced.

> **LANGUAGE TIP**
> There is no *st-* sound in Thai, nor a *v* sound. Thais commonly put a short **a** vowel between the **s** and **t** when pronouncing English words that begin with this combination (e.g. **sa-top**, **sa-tart**), while *v* is pronounced as **f** or, by some speakers, **p**.

 01.03 *Somchai is saying hello to a teacher called Somjit.*

3 What word does Somchai use before Somjit's name?

Somchai	สวัสดีครับอาจารย์สมจิตต์	sa-wùt dee krúp ah-jahn Sŏm-jìt
Somjit	สวัสดีค่ะ	sa-wùt dee kà

> **LANGUAGE TIP**
> The word **ah-jahn** (*teacher, lecturer*) is used instead of **kOOn** when addressing teachers, college lecturers, sports coaches and others with specialist knowledge. If you don't know the teacher's name, then **ah-jahn** on its own is quite sufficient.

 01.04 *Somchai is saying goodbye to Somjit.*

4 How does Somjit respond?

Somchai	ผมไปละนะครับอาจารย์	pŏm bpai lá ná krúp, ah-jahn
Somjit	ค่ะ	kà

 01.05 *Wanpen is saying goodbye to Steve.*

5 How does Steve respond?

Wanpen	ฉันไปละนะคะ	chún bpai lá ná ká
Steve	ครับ	krúp

Language discovery 2

PARTICLES

Particles are untranslateable words; some convey the mood of the speaker, while others have a grammatical purpose, such as indicating that the sentence is a question or a command.

Which polite particles have you met in this unit so far?

Male speakers use **krúp** (high tone) both at the end of a statement and at the end of a question. Female speakers use **kà** (low tone) or **kâh** (falling tone) at the end of a statement and **ká** (high tone) at the end of a question. We have met just one example of the particle **ká**, In the expression **chún bpai lá ná ká** (*I'm off now, right?*). The word **ná** in this phrase is a question particle, rather like *right?* or *OK?* at the end of a statement in English. You don't need to use polite particles at the end of every single sentence, but inserting them at regular intervals indicates that you are being polite and respectful to the person you are talking to. It's important to get used to using them so that you don't sound abrupt or disrespectful.

Conversation 2: *Thank you* and *sorry*

 01.06 Wanpen is thanking Somjit.

1 How does Somjit respond to Wanpen's thanks?

Wanpen	ขอบคุณค่ะอาจารย์	kòrp-kOOn kà, ah-jahn
Somjit	ไม่เป็นไรค่ะ	mâi bpen rai kà

 01.07 *Steve is thanking Somchai.*

2 How does Somchai acknowledge Steve's thanks?

Steve	ขอบคุณมากครับ	kòrp-kOOn mâhk krúp
Somchai	ครับ	krúp

> **LANGUAGE TIP**
> The word for *thank you* in Thai is **kòrp-kOOn**. You can respond to thanks with either **mâi bpen rai** (*you're welcome*), or just the polite particle **krúp** or **kà/kâh**, which we might translate as *sure* or *that's OK*. If you want to say *thank you very much* you can add **mâhk** (*very, much*) after **kòrp-kOOn**.

 01.08 *Steve is apologizing to Wanpen.*

3 How does Wanpen respond to Steve's apology?

Steve	ขอโทษครับ	kŏr-tôht krúp
Wanpen	ไม่เป็นไรค่ะ	mâi bpen rai kà

> **LANGUAGE TIP**
> When you want to apologize, you say **kŏr-tôht**. The normal response to an apology is **mâi bpen rai**.

4 In which other situation can we use mâi bpen rai?

 5 Now listen to the conversations again and repeat. Be sure to pay attention to the pronunciation.

💡 Language discovery 3

mâi bpen rai

mâi bpen rai can be used in response to both thanks and apologies. Hardly surprising then, that some Thais smile and say *Never mind!* when you thank them. Many Western scholars writing on Thailand in the post-World War II period saw this phrase as neatly encapsulating Thais' outlook on life, and it appears in the title of a frequently re-printed memoir of expatriate life in Bangkok in the early 1960s, *Mai pen rai means Never Mind*.

🔓 Practice

1 **Let's check some of the key points you have learned in this unit:**
   a Somjit is a teacher. How would you address her?
   b Somchai is a work colleague. How would you address him?
   c What is the difference between **pŏm** and **chún**?
   d What is the difference between **kà** and **ká**?

2 **Fill in the correct male and female polite particles in the following exchanges:**

   a **Wanpen**   sa-wùt dee _____ kOOn Sa-dteef.
     Steve   sa-wùt dee _____

   b **Steve**   pŏm bpai lá ná _____
     Wanpen   _____

   c **Somjit**   chún bpai lá ná _____
     Sue   _____

   d **Steve**   kòrp-kOOn mâhk _____, ah-jahn.
     Somjit   mâi bpen rai _____

   e **Sue**   kŏr-tôht _____
     Somchai mâi bpen rai _____

3 **What would you say ...**
   a ... if you were greeting a teacher?
   b ... if you wanted to leave, or say goodbye?
   c ... if you wanted to thank someone very much?
   d ... if you accidentally bumped into someone?
   e ... if a waitress spilt water on your table?

4 **How would you respond if a Thai said the following?**
   a sa-wùt dee kà
   b pŏm bpai lá ná krúp
   c kòrp-kOOn mâhk kà
   d kŏr-tôht krúp

 Pronunciation

 1 01.09 **Listen to the audio and repeat after the speaker, paying special attention to the tones.**

krúp	dee krúp	wùt dee krúp	sa-wùt dee krúp
kà	dee kà	wùt dee kà	sa-wùt dee kà
krúp	ná krúp	bpai lá ná krúp	
ká	ná ká	bpai lá ná ká	
krúp	kòrp-kOOn krúp	kà	kòrp-kOOn kà
krúp	kŏr-tôht krúp	kà	kŏr-tôht kà

 2 01.10 **Now listen to the names of the Thai characters in this unit and repeat them. Pay special attention to getting the tones correct.**

Wun-pen	Wun-pen	Wun-pen
Sŏm-jìt	Sŏm-jìt	Sŏm-jìt
Sŏm-chai:	Sŏm-chai:	Sŏm-chai:

Reading and writing

 You're not going to learn Thai letters in the normal alphabetical order (which might surprise or shock your Thai friends). If you were to do so, you would waste a lot of time in Unit 3 learning some very rarely used letters. Instead the letters are presented in manageable groups, dealing with the most commonly occurring letters first.

Thai consonants are divided into three classes – *low class*, *mid class* and *high class*. It is essential to remember which class a consonant belongs to as the class of the initial consonant in a word will play a part in determining the tone of that word.

All the consonants in this lesson are *low class* consonants. They are all pronounced with an inherent **-or** sound.

 01.11 **Listen to the audio and practise writing the letters following the order of strokes shown.**

| n | m | ng | r | l | y | w |

Vowels are either long or short. It is important to know whether a vowel is long or short because this will influence the tone of the word, as you will discover in Unit 4.

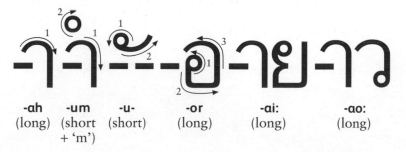

| **-ah** (long) | **-um** (short + 'm') | **-u-** (short) | **-or** (long) | **-ai:** (long) | **-ao:** (long) |

We're going to put some letters together now to form some simple words. We haven't given you the meanings of these words because at this stage we just want you to feel comfortable reading the Thai letters.

 01.12 First, listen to the audio and look at the words at the same time. Next, copy out the Thai words (preferably several times). Then cover up the Romanized transcription and read the Thai words, first going across the rows, then down the columns and finally picking out words at random.

นา	มา	ลา	ยา
nah	**mah**	**lah**	**yah**

วาง	ยาง	งาน	งาม
wahng	**yahng**	**ngahn**	**ngahm**

นำ	รำ	ลำ	ยำ
num	**rum**	**lum**	**yum**

มัน	ยัง	วัน	ลัง
mun	**yung**	**wun**	**lung**

รอ	นอน	ยอม	มอง
ror	**norn**	**yorm**	**morng**

นาย	ยาย	ราว	ลาว
nai:	**yai:**	**rao:**	**lao:**

Make sure that you can read all of these words confidently before attempting the Reading and Writing section in the next unit.

Test yourself

🎧 **01.13 Listen to the audio and check your answers in the Answer Key.**

1 How would you say …?

a	Hello	**d**	You're welcome!
b	Goodbye	**e**	I'm sorry
c	Thank you	**f**	Never mind, don't worry!

2 How would you respond if a Thai said …?

a	sa-wùt dee krúp	**c**	kòrp-kOOn krúp
b	bpai lá ná krúp	**d**	kŏr-tôht kà

3 What class are these consonants?

น   ม   ง   ร   ล   ย   ว

4 How would you read the following words?

a	มา	**d**	นอน
b	รำ	**e**	ยาย
c	ยัง	**f**	ลาว

5 Here is a sample of Thai script. Notice that there are no spaces between words and that there are symbols above and below some letters. These are either vowel symbols or tone marks. Underline any letters that you can now recognize. Don't worry if there are symbols above or underneath the letter. The first line has been done for you.

เล็กแต่งงานที่กรุงเทพฯ ค่ะ สามีเป็นคนอังกฤษ
เคยทำงานที่บริษัทใหญ่แห่งหนึ่งแถวถนนสุขุมวิท
เรากลับมาอยู่ที่อังกฤษเมื่อสามปีก่อน
ความจริงเล็กไม่อยากมาอยู่อังกฤษเลย

SELF CHECK	
I CAN…	
○	…say *hello* and *goodbye*.
○	…say *thank you* and *you're welcome*.
○	…say *sorry* and *never mind/don't worry about it*.
○	…use polite particles.
○	…recognize the most common low class consonants and read some simple words.

2 kOOn chêu: a-rai?

What's your name?

In this unit you will learn how to:
▶ *state your name, nationality and place of origin.*
▶ *ask someone's name, nationality and place of origin.*
▶ *recognize the most common mid class consonants.*
▶ *read some words and two place names.*

CEFR: *(A1) Can introduce him/herself and ask and answer simple questions about where he/she comes from.*

Bangkok and beyond

While you may often have to answer the question, **kOOn bpen kon châht a-rai?** (*What nationality are you?*), you will only rarely ask this question yourself. It's more useful to be able to ask Thais whether they come from **grOOng-tâyp** (*Bangkok*), or which **pâhk** (*region*) or **jung-wùt** (*province*) they come from.

grOOng-tâyp, often written as **Krungthep** in guidebooks, is a much abbreviated form of the enormously long official title. Thailand is divided into 76 provinces which are distributed across four regions, with each region having its own distinct dialect and local customs and cuisine. The four regions are:

ภาคกลาง	**pâhk glahng**	*the Central Region*
ภาคใต้	**pâhk dtâi:**	*the South*
ภาคเหนือ	**pâhk nĕu-a**	*the North*
ภาคอีสาน	**pâhk ee-sŏhn**	*the Northeast*

A person's nationality, regional identity and home province can be expressed using **kon** (*person*) followed by the name of the country, region or province:

คนไทย	**kon tai**	*a Thai (person)*
คนภาคเหนือ	**kon pâhk nĕu-a**	*a northerner*
คนเชียงใหม่	**kon chee-ung mài**	*a person from Chiangmai*

 How do you think you describe someone who comes from Bangkok?

Vocabulary builder

02.01 **Listen to the audio and repeat each word after the speaker. Try to think about the tone that you are hearing as you listen.**

TALKING ABOUT YOURSELF

คุณ	kOOn	*you*
ชื่อ	chêu:	*first name; to have the first name …*
อะไร	a-rai	*what?*
ดิฉัน	di-chún	*I (female, formal)*
ใช่ไหม	châi mái?	*…, is that right?*
ใช่	châi	*yes to a* **châi mái?** *question*
เป็น	bpen	*to be*
คน	kon	*person*
ชาติ	châht	*nation*
อังกฤษ	ung-grìt	*English*
กรุงเทพฯ	grOOng-tâyp	*Bangkok*

NEW EXPRESSIONS

คุณชื่ออะไร	kOOn chêu: a-rai?	*What's your name?*
ดิฉันชื่อ ... ค่ะ	di-chún chêu: … kà	*My (female) name is …*
คุณเป็นคนชาติอะไร	kOOn bpen kon châht a-rai?	*What nationality are you?*

 How do English and Thai differ in where they place the *what?* question word?

Conversations

 02.02 *Steve is talking to a Thai girl.*

1 What is the girl's name?

Steve	ขอโทษคุณชื่ออะไรครับ	kǒr-tôht kOOn chêu: a-rai krúp?
Thai	ดิฉันชื่อ มาลิกาค่ะ	di-chún chêu: Mah-li-gah kà
Steve	คุณมาลิกาใช่ไหมครับ	kOOn Mah-li-gah châi mái krúp?
Thai	ใช่ค่ะ	châi kà

2 Read and listen to the conversation again and answer these questions.

  a How does Steve begin his first question?

  b How does the girl say *I*?

  c What does Steve say to check that he has heard correctly?

  d How does the girl say *yes*?

> **LANGUAGE TIP**
> In the previous unit we met **kǒr-tôht**, meaning *sorry*. It is also used to make personal questions sound more polite.

 02.03 *Somjit and Steve are asking each other where they come from.*

3 Does Somjit come from Bangkok?

Somjit	ขอโทษ	kǒr-tôht
	คุณสตีฟเป็นคนชาติอะไรคะ	kOOn Sa-dteef bpen kon châht a-rai ká?
Steve	ผมเป็นคนอังกฤษครับ	pǒm bpen kon ung-grìt krúp
	ขอโทษ	kǒr-tôht
	อาจารย์เป็นคนกรุงเทพฯ	ah-jahn bpen kon grOOng-tâyp
	ใช่ไหมครับ	châi mái krúp?
Somjit	ไม่ใช่ค่ะ	mâi châi kà
	เป็นคนภาคเหนือค่ะ	bpen kon pâhk něu-a kà
Steve	จังหวัดอะไรครับ	jung-wùt a-rai krúp?
Somjit	จังหวัดลำปางค่ะ	jung-wùt lum-bpahng kà

4 Read and listen to the conversation again and answer these questions.

  a How does Somjit address Steve?   **c** How does Steve address Somjit?

  b What nationality is Steve?   **d** Where does Somjit come from?

Language discovery

kOOn (*you*) is a rather formal pronoun which establishes a sense of respect and polite distance. Somjit and Steve know each other already and deliberately avoid using it when addressing each other. a. What do they say instead? b. And when Somjit says, **bpen kon pâhk něu-a kà**, what word has she deliberately omitted?

1 PERSONAL PRONOUNS

02.04 There are many more personal pronouns in Thai than in English, and they can be used to convey different levels of formality, status, and intimacy between speakers. However, you can get by quite effectively with a limited number of pronouns, the most useful of which are:

ผม	**pǒm**	*I (male)*	คุณ	**kOOn**	*you (singular and plural)*
ดิฉัน	**di-chún**	*I (female, formal)*	เขา	**káo**	*he, she, they*
ฉัน	**chún**	*I (female, informal)*	เรา	**rao**	*we*

Names, often preceded by the polite title **kOOn**, and occupations (e.g. **ah-jahn**) can also be used as pronouns.

A very common feature of Thai is to omit a pronoun when it is clear who is speaking, being addressed or referred to. Thus, **bpen kon châht a-rai?** could mean *What's your nationality?* or *What's his/her/their nationality?*, while **bpen kon tai**, could mean *I'm Thai* or *He's/she's/they're Thai*. English-speaking learners sometimes fear that if they abandon pronouns, their language will rapidly descend into chaos and become incomprehensible. It won't! It will just sound more like Thai. In many of the examples used in this book, you will see that there is no pronoun in the Thai to match the English translation. This is deliberate!

2 WHAT?

The Thai word for *what?* is **a-rai**. It normally occurs at the end of the sentence. Answers to these questions are formed by replacing **a-rai** with the appropriate piece of information. Note that the word **châht** (*nation*) is omitted in the answer to a question about nationality:

> kǒr-tôht kOOn
> chêu: a-rai?

> di-chún chêu:
> Mah-li-gah kà

คุณชื่ออะไร
What's your name?

ดิฉันชื่อ มาลิกาค่ะ
My name is Malika.

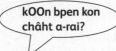

kOOn bpen kon
châht a-rai?

pǒm bpen kon
ung-grìt krúp

คุณเป็นคนชาติอะไร
What nationality are you?

ผมเป็นคนอังกฤษครับ
I'm English.

3 THE VERB *TO BE*

bpen is one of several different Thai verbs that are used to translate
is/are, was/were etc. **bpen** does have other meanings, but when it means
to be, it is always followed by a noun:

| ผมเป็นคนอังกฤษ | pǒm bpen kon ung-grìt | *I'm English.* |
| เขาเป็นคนภาคเหนือ | káo bpen kon pâhk něu-a | *She's a northerner.* |

In negative sentences like, *I'm not a …*, **mâi châi …** is used instead of
a negative word with **bpen**:

ฉันไม่ใช่คนกรุงเทพฯ	chún mâi châi kon grOOng-tâyp
	I'm not from Bangkok.
เขาไม่ใช่คนอเมริกัน	káo mâi châi kon a-may-ri-gun
	He's not an American.

4 … châi mái? QUESTIONS

The question particle **châi mái?** is tagged
onto the end of a statement to transform
it into a confirmation-seeking question, like
… isn't it?, … don't they?, etc. in English. It is very useful for checking
that you have heard or understood something correctly. The answer to
a **… châi mái?** question is either **châi** (*yes*) or **mâi châi** (*no*):

> **LANGUAGE TIP**
> Remember, you cannot put
> **mâi** (*not*) before **bpen** to mean
> *is not …*; use **mâi châi** instead.

kOOn Mah-li-gah
châi mái?

châi kà

คุณมาลิกาใช่ไหม
Khun Malika, right?

ใช่ค่ะ
Yes.

bpen kon grOOng-
tâyp châi mái?

mâi châi

เป็นคนกรุงเทพฯใช่ไหม
You're from Bangkok, aren't you?

ไม่ใช่
No.

> **LANGUAGE TIP**
> WARNING! There are several
> ways of saying *yes* and *no* in
> Thai. **châi** is the correct way
> to say *yes* to a **châi mái?**
> question, but it cannot be
> used to say *yes* whenever
> you feel like it! In the lessons
> that follow, we'll learn more
> ways of saying *yes* and *no*.

ⓘ Practice

1 Fill in the missing words in the following exchanges:

a **Steve** kŏr-tôht kOOn chêu: Malika châi mái krúp?

Malika _____ kà

b **Somjit** kOOn Sue bpen kon _____ a-rai ká?

Sue bpen _____ a-may-ri-gun kà

c **Sue** ah-jahn bpen kon _____ a-rai ká?

Somjit jung-wùt lum-bpahng kà

d **Steve** kŏr-tôht, kOOn chêu: Sŏm-chai: châi mái krúp?

Somchok _____ krúp. chêu: Sŏm-chôhk krúp

2 What would you say …

a … if you wanted to ask someone their name?

b … if you wanted to ask someone their nationality?

c … if you wanted to ask a Thai if they came from Bangkok?

d … if you wanted to ask a Thai if they came from the South?

e … if you wanted to ask a Thai what province they came from?

3 How would you respond if a Thai asked you the following?

a kOOn chêu: a-rai ká?

b kOOn bpen kon châht a-rai ká?

c kOOn bpen kon a-may-ri-gun châi mái ká?

d kOOn bpen kon pâhk dtâi: châi mái ká?

4 Match the following questions and answers:

a káo chêu Su-dteef châi mái?   1 mâi châi bpen kon grOOng tâyp

b káo bpen kon châht a-rai?   2 châi

c kOOn bpen kon ung-grìt châi mái?   3 bpen kon tai

d bpen kon pâhk nĕu-a châi mái?   4 mâi châi bpen kon a-may-ri-gun

Pronunciation

 02.05 **Listen to the audio and repeat after the speaker, paying special attention to the tones.**

krúp	a-rai krúp	chêu: a-rai krúp	kOOn chêu: a-rai krúp?
ká	a-rai ká	chêu: a-rai ká	kOOn chêu: a-rai ká?
krúp	mái krúp	châi mái krúp	grOOng-tâyp châi mái krúp
ká	mái ká	châi mái ká	grOOng-tâyp châi mái ká

Go further

 1 02.06 **We've seen that a person's nationality can be stated by using kon (*person*) followed by the name of the country. Here are some more examples. Listen to them on the audio and repeat.**

คนอังกฤษ	**kon ung-grìt**	*English*
คนไทย	**kon tai**	*Thai*
คนอเมริกัน	**kon a-may-ri-gun**	*American*
คนจีน	**kon jeen**	*Chinese*
คนญี่ปุ่น	**kon yêe-bpÒOn**	*Japanese*
คนเกาหลี	**kon gao-lĕe**	*Korean*
คนฝรั่งเศส	**kon fa-rung-sàyt**	*French*

Names of countries are normally preceded by the word **bpra-tâyt** (*country*), but Thailand is often referred to by the more colloquial term, **meu-ung tai**. **meu-ung** can mean *country* or *city*.

ประเทศอังกฤษ	**bpra-tâyt ung-grìt**	*England*
ประเทศอเมริกา	**bpra-tâyt a-may-ri-gah**	*America*
ประเทศจีน	**bpra-tâyt jeen**	*China*
ประเทศญี่ปุ่น	**bpra-tâyt yêe-bpÒOn**	*Japan*
ประเทศเกาหลี	**bpra-tâyt gao-lĕe**	*Korea*
ประเทศฝรั่งเศส	**bpra-tâyt fa-rung-sàyt**	*France*
ประเทศไทย	**bpra-tâyt tai**	*Thailand*
เมืองไทย	**meu-ung tai**	*Thailand*

 2 **What countries do you think these are:**

a ประเทศไอร์แลนด์ bpra-tâyt ai-lairn

b ประเทศรัสเซีย bpra-tâyt rút-see-a

c ประเทศเบลเยียม bpra-tâyt bayl-yee-um

> **LANGUAGE TIP**
> The names of many countries are basically Thai pronunciations of the English name.

Reading and writing

All of the consonants in this unit are mid class consonants. Just like the consonants in the last unit, they are pronounced with an inherent **-or** vowel.

1 02.07 **Listen to the audio and practise writing the letters following the order of strokes shown.**

ก	จ	ด	ต	บ	ป	อ
g	j	d	dt	b	bp	('zero')

Don't worry if you can't hear the difference between **d** and **dt**, and **b** and **bp** at this stage; it will come with practice, as your ears become more attuned to the sounds of Thai.

Notice that the final symbol in this group is identical in appearance to the vowel **-or** you learned in the last unit. When the symbol occurs at the beginning of a word, however, it is a consonant, which we can call 'zero' consonant because it has no inherent sound of its own. It is used when writing words which begin with a vowel sound:

อาง	อัน	อำ	ออ	อาย	อาว
ahng	un	um	or	ai:	ao:

2 02.08 **Here are some words using the new consonants and the vowels you learned in Unit 1.**

All of these words, like those in Unit 1, are pronounced with a mid-tone. Listen to the audio and follow in the book. Try reading along with the audio; then cover up the transcription and work across the rows and up and down the columns until you are confident that you can read these words accurately; finally, practise copying them out, reading each word out loud as you do so. Don't worry about the meanings of these words; the important thing at this stage is simply to be able to relate correct sounds to letters.

กัน	กาว	จาน	จอง
gun	gao:	jahn	jorng

จำ	จัง	ดำ	ดัง
jum	jung	dum	dung

ดารา	ตาย	ตาม	บาง
dah-rah	dtai:	dtahm	bahng

VOWELS

In the previous unit we met one vowel symbol that appeared above a consonant rather than following it on the same line. In this unit we have vowel symbols that are written in front of, on top of, and beneath the consonant. Remember that the dash indicates the position of the consonant.

 3 02.09 **Look at the following examples carefully and then listen to the audio. The first two vowels are pronounced exactly the same, but they are not interchangeable in writing; the correct spelling of a word has to be memorized.**

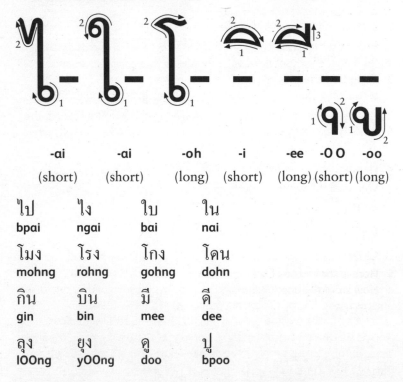

-ai	-ai	-oh	-i	-ee	-oo	-oo
(short)	(short)	(long)	(short)	(long)	(short)	(long)
ไป	ไง	ใบ	ใน			
bpai	ngai	bai	nai			
โมง	โรง	โกง	โดน			
mohng	rohng	gohng	dohn			
กิน	บิน	มี	ดี			
gin	bin	mee	dee			
ลุง	ยุง	ดู	ปู			
lOOng	yOOng	doo	bpoo			

LANGUAGE TIP

It's a good idea to write down all the letters, as you learn them, on a single piece of paper and keep it close at hand when you are reading Thai words. It will help you to remember the letters and also save you from the inconvenience of having to turn back pages if you can't remember a certain letter.

🔎 Test yourself

1 **Let's check some of the key points you have learned in this unit:**
   a Why might you begin a question with **kŏr-tôht**?
   b When do you use a … **châi mái** question?
   c What are the two possible answers to a … **châi mái** question?
   d What is the Thai name for Bangkok?
   e What is the difference between **pâhk** and **jung-wùt**?

2 **How would you say the following?**
   a Excuse me, what's your name?
   b Excuse me, are you from Bangkok?
   c Excuse me, what province are you from?
   d She is from the North, not Bangkok.

3 **Complete the sentences.**
   a ah-jahn Sŏm-jìt _____ kon grOOng-tâyp, bpen kon pâhk nĕu-a.
   b kOOn Sa-dteef bpen kon ung-grìt, _____ kon a-may-ri-gun.

4 What class are these consonants?

ก   จ   ด   ต   บ   ป   อ

5 **Here are some common words with their meanings. How would you read them?**

   a มี   *to have*   d ดู   *to look at*
   b ไป   *to go*   e ใน   *in*
   c กิน   *to eat*   f ดี   *good*

6 **Here is the name of a European city and a Thai province. How would you read them?**

ลอนดอน   ลำปาง

SELF CHECK

	I CAN...
◯	…state my name, nationality and place of origin.
◯	…ask someone's name, nationality and place of origin.
◯	…recognize the most common mid class consonants.
◯	…read some simple words.

3 têe-nêe mee in-dter-net kah-fây mái?

Is there an internet café here?

In this unit you will learn how to:
▶ *ask for simple directions.*
▶ *count from one to ten.*
▶ *recognize the most common high class consonants.*
▶ *read a simple conversation.*

CEFR: *(A1) Can ask for directions and recognize and use basic phrases describing a location in relation to its surroundings.*

◉ Getting around

Getting about on foot provides an opportunity to see things that you would otherwise miss if travelling by public transport. While free maps of Bangkok are available at the airport, they tend to show only a limited part of the centre. More detailed maps, some showing bus routes, others full of suggestions of off-beat places to visit, are readily available in bookstores selling English-language books. Be aware, however, that many local residents and taxi drivers have never seen a map of their city and they will struggle to give directions using a map thrust under their nose.

Asking for directions is a good way to practise your Thai. You can rehearse the question carefully and then try it out any number of times on passers-by. In this lesson we learn three different question, **têe-nêe mee … mái?** (*Is there a … here?*), the less-specific **tǎir-o née mee … mái?** (*Is there a … around here?*) and the straightforward **… yòo têe-nǎi?** (*Where is …?*).

03.01 Listen to the audio and try to imitate the speakers as closely as you can. Use the Romanized Thai words to help you focus on the tone that you are hearing and trying to produce.

DIRECTIONS

ที่นี่	têe nêe	here
มี	mee	there is/are; to have
อินเตอร์เนตคาเฟ่	in-dter-net kah-fây	internet café
ไหม	mái?	question particle used in yes/no questions
อยู่	yòo	to be situated at
ชั้น	chún	floor; storey
ห้า	hâh	five
แถวนี้	tǎir-o née	around here, in this area
ธนาคาร	ta-na-kahn	bank
ที่โน่น	têe nôhn	over there
ไกล	glai	far, to be far
ไม่	mâi	not
ใกล้ ๆ	glâi glâi	near, to be near
ไปรษณีย์	bprai-sa-nee	post office
ห้องน้ำ	hôrng náhm	toilet
ที่ไหน	têe-nǎi?	where?
ข้างหลัง	kûng lǔng	behind, at the back
ซ้าย	sái:	left

NEW EXPRESSIONS

อะไรนะ	a-rai ná?	*Pardon? What was that again?*
ที่นี่มี ...ไหม	têe nêe mee … mái?	*Is there a … here?*
อยู่ชั้น ...	yòo chún …	*It's on the … floor*
ชั้นอะไรนะ	chún a-rai ná?	*What floor did you say?*
แถวนี้มี ...ไหม	tăir-o née mee … mái?	*Is there a … around here?*
อยู่ที่โน่น	yòo têe nôhn	*It's over there*
ไกลไหม	glai mái?	*Is it far?*
อยู่ใกล้ ๆ ...	yòo glâi glâi …	*It's near …*
... อยู่ที่ไหน	… yòo têe-năi?	*Where is …?*
อยู่ข้างหลัง	yòo kûng lŭng	*It's at the back*
ทางซ้าย	tahng sái:	*on the left*

Conversations

 03.02 *Sue is in a shopping mall.*

1 What is Sue looking for?

Sue	ขอโทษค่ะ	kŏr-tôht kà
	ที่นี่มีอินเตอร์เนตคาเฟ่ไหมคะ	têe nêe mee in-dter-net kah-fây mái ká?
Thai	มีค่ะ	mee kà
	อยู่ชั้นห้า	yòo chún hâh
Sue	ชั้นอะไรนะคะ	chún a-rai ná ká?
Thai	ชั้นห้าค่ะ	chún hâh kà
Sue	ขอบคุณมากค่ะ	kòrp-kOOn mâhk kà
Thai	ไม่เป็นไรค่ะ	mâi bpen rai kà

2 **Read and listen to the conversation again and answer these questions.**

  a What floor will Sue have to go to?
  b Which word did Sue have difficulty hearing?
  c How did she ask the Thai to say the word again?

 03.03 *Steve stops a passer-by in the street.*

3 **Is there a bank around here?**

Steve	ขอโทษครับ	kŏr-tôht krúp
	แถวนี้มีธนาคารไหม	tăir-o née mee ta-na-kahn mái?
Thai	มีครับ	mee krúp
	อยู่ที่โน่น	yòo têe nôhn
Steve	ไกลไหมครับ	glai mái krúp?
Thai	ไม่ไกลครับ	mâi glai krúp
	อยู่ใกล้ ๆ ไปรษณีย์	yòo glâi glâi bprai-sa-nee
Steve	ขอบคุณครับ	kòrp-kOOn krúp
Thai	ครับ	krúp

4 **Read and listen to the conversation again and answer these questions.**

  a How does the Thai describe the location of the bank?
  b How does the Thai respond when Steve asks, **glai mái krúp**?
  c What is it near?

> **LANGUAGE TIP**
> Be careful not to confuse the question word **mái?** pronounced with a high tone, with the negative word, **mâi**, pronounced with a falling tone.

5 Where is the toilet?

Steve	ขอโทษครับ	kŏr-tôht krúp
	ห้องน้ำอยู่ที่ไหนครับ	hôrng náhm yòo têe-năi krúp?
Waitress	อยู่ข้างหลังค่ะ	yòo kûng lŭng kà
	ทางซ้าย	tahng sái:
Steve	ทางซ้ายใช่ไหมครับ	tahng sái: châi mái krúp?
Waitress	ใช่ค่ะ	châi kà
Steve	ขอบคุณครับ	kòrp-kOOn krúp
Waitress	ค่ะ	kà

6 Read and listen to the conversation again and answer these questions.

a What's the Thai word for *where*? Does it come at the beginning or the end of a sentence?

b The waitress gives two pieces of information about the location of the toilet. Which piece of information does Steve have to check that he has heard correctly?

c What does he say to check that he has heard correctly?

💡 Language discovery

1 ... mái? QUESTIONS

1 Look at Conversations 1 and 2 and find the three questions that end in mái? How are the questions answered?

The question particle **mái?** occurs at the end of a sentence and is used in questions requiring a yes/no answer. **mái?** questions are neutral; they do not anticipate the answer, unlike the confirmation-seeking question **châi mái?** (Unit 2).

To answer *yes* to a **mái?** question, the verb in the question is repeated; to answer *no*, use **mâi** + VERB:

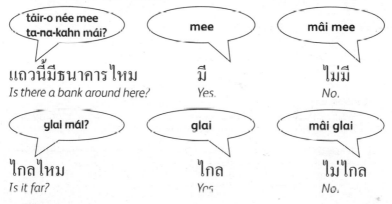

tâir-o née mee ta-na-kahn mái?	**mee**	**mâi mee**
แถวนี้มีธนาคารไหม	มี	ไม่มี
Is there a bank around here?	*Yes.*	*No.*
glai mái?	**glai**	**mâi glai**
ไกลไหม	ไกล	ไม่ไกล
Is it far?	*Yes.*	*No.*

2 NUMBERS 1–10

2 Look at Conversation 1 again. What floor was the internet café located on?

 3 03.05 Listen to numbers 1–10 on the audio. Both Thai and Arabic numbers are in common everyday use, so it is important to be able to recognize Thai numbers.

๑	๒	๓	๔	๕
nèung	sŏrng	săhm	sèe	hâh
1	2	3	4	5

๖	๗	๘	๙	๑๐
hòk	jèt	bpàirt	gâo:	sìp
6	7	8	9	10

3 PARDON?

The simplest way to get someone to repeat something is to say **a-rai ná** (*Pardon?*). But using it as often as you actually need to will neither enhance your credibility as a Thai speaker, nor your self-confidence. In the first conversation in this unit, Sue demonstrates a slightly more sophisticated and focused way of getting someone to repeat something. She manages to hear the word **chún**, but not the word **hâh**. So instead of just saying **a-rai ná** (*Pardon?*), she is able to ask **chún a-rai ná** (*Which floor was that you said?*), which (a) sends out a clear message that she is understanding something, (b) tells the Thai which word to repeat particularly clearly, and (c) leaves Sue with a feel-good factor that the simpler **a-rai ná** could never have matched!

4 WHERE?

The question word **têe-nǎi?** (*where?*) always occurs at the end of a sentence in Thai. When asking where something is, it follows the verb **yòo** (*to be situated at*):

ห้องน้ำอยู่ที่ไหน	**hôrng náhm yòo têe-nǎi?**	*Where's the toilet?*
ไปรษณีย์อยู่ที่ไหน	**bprai-sa-nee yòo têe-nǎi?**	*Where's the post office?*

> **LANGUAGE TIP**
> When you want to ask *where?* questions with the verb **bpai** (*to go*), the **têe** in **têe-nǎi?** is usually dropped:
>
> ไปไหน   **bpai nǎi?**   *Where are you going?*

5 REDUPLICATION

4 When the passer-by told Steve (Conversation 3) that the bank was near the post office, how did he express the idea of *near*?

The repetition, or **reduplication**, of an adjective or adverb is a common feature of spoken Thai, widely celebrated on t-shirts bearing the slogan, *Same, same …* on the front, and *… but different* on the back. It is often wrongly assumed that reduplication automatically intensifies the meaning, the equivalent to putting *very* in front of the adjective. A more common function of reduplication is to make the meaning of the reduplicated word less precise; it often corresponds to the English use of *-ish*. But had the t-shirt designer opted for *Similar* – a more accurate translation of the Thai – on the front, who would have bought it? So when we say something **yòo glâi glâi …**, we mean it is *near-ish*, or *fairly near*, not *very near*.

Practice

1 **How would you say the following?**

   a Excuse me, is there a bank around here?   **c** Is there a toilet here?

   b Where is the post office?   **d** Is it far?

2 **How would you dial these telephone numbers?**

   a ๐๘๕๖๗๒๔๕   **b** ๐๘๖๗๓๓๖๐   **c** ๐๒๓๓๗๔๗๒

3 **What is the difference between** *(a) near* **and** *(b) far* **in Thai?**

4 **Read the following exchange. Steve is listening to directions, but he doesn't hear the last word. What should he say?**

Thai	yòo glâi glâi bprai-sa-nee
Steve	yòo glâi glâi …

 Pronunciation

 03.06 **Listen to the audio and repeat after the speaker.**

năi ká?   têe-năi ká?   yòo têe-năi ká?   hôrng náhm yòo têe-năi ká?

năi ká?   têe-năi ká?   yòo têe-năi ká?   ta-na-kahn yòo têe-năi ká?

năi ká?   têe-năi ká?   yòo têe-năi ká?   bprai-sa-nee yòo têe-năi ká?

Go further

03.07 In the Conversation, you heard a waitress telling Steve that the toilet was **kûng lŭng** (*at the back*) and **tahng sái:** (*on the left*). **kûng** occurs in a number of location words, while **tahng** also occurs with **kwăh** (*right*). **Listen to the new expressions on the audio and repeat them.**

ข้างบน	**kûng bon**	*on; upstairs*
ข้างล่าง	**kûng lâhng**	*under; downstairs*
ข้างหลัง	**kûng lŭng**	*behind*
ข้างหน้า	**kûng nâh**	*in front (of)*
ข้างใน	**kûng nai**	*in; inside*
ข้างนอก	**kûng nôrk**	*outside*
ทางขวา	**tahng kwăh**	*on the right*

Reading and writing

03.08 All the new consonants in this unit are high class consonants. High class consonants are pronounced with an inherent rising tone, so the following letters are read, **kǒr**, **chǒr**, **tǒr**, **pǒr**, etc. Notice that there are three different high class **s** symbols. The most common is the third, while the first two appear mainly in words of foreign origin.

ข	ฉ	ถ	ผ	ฝ
k	ch	t	p	f

ศ	ษ	ส	ห
s	s	s	h

Here are some words beginning with the new high-class consonants for you to practise reading:

ขอ	ของ	ฉาย	ถาม
kǒr	kǒrng	chǎi:	tǎhm

ถุง	ผอม	ผี	ฝา
tǒOng	pǒrm	pěe	fǎh

สาว	สอน	หา	หู
sǎo:	sǒrn	hǎh	hǒo

SILENT ห AT THE BEGINNING OF A WORD

There are a number of words in Thai spelt with an initial ห which is not pronounced. The function of this 'silent' ห is to convert the low class consonant that follows into a high class consonant. Such words then follow the tone rules of words with that begin with a high class consonant.

หมอ	หวาน	หลาย	หนี	หมู	ไหน
mǒr	wǎhn	lǎi:	něe	mǒo	nǎi

Note that the question particle **mái?**, which we meet in this lesson, is written as if it should be pronounced with a rising tone, but in normal speech it is actually pronounced with a high tone:

ไหม	mái?

Test yourself

🎧 **03.09 Listen to the audio and check your answers in the Answer Key.**

1 **How would you translate the following:**
   a tăir-o née mee ta-na-kahn mái?
   b tăir-o née mee ta-na-kahn châi mái?

2 **How would you say yes and no to the following questions:**
   a têe nêe mee in-dter-net kah-fây mái?
   b glai mái?   **c** yòo tahng sái: châi mái?

3 **How would you say the following?**
   a Excuse me, is there a toilet around here?
   b Where is the post office?   **c** Is there a bank here?

4 **Here are some more common words. Read them first and then listen to the audio to check whether you were right.**
   a ของ of   **d** หมอ doctor
   b ถุง bag   **e** หลาย several
   c หา to visit   **f** ไหน where?

5 **Where is Somchai going?**

| Wanpen | ไปไหน |
| Somchai | ไปหาหมอ |

6 **Who is Wanpen going to visit? Is Somchai going too?**

Wanpen	ไปไหม
Somchai	ไปไหน
Wanpen	ไปหามาลิกา
Somchai	ไป

SELF CHECK

	I CAN...
○	...ask for simple directions.
○	...count from one to ten.
○	...recognize the most common high class consonants.
○	...read a simple conversational exchange.

1 Fill in the missing question word in these exchanges:

   a Thai   kOOn bpen kon a-may-ri-gun _____ ká?

       Foreigner   mâi châi krúp bpen kon ung-grìt

   b Foreigner   kOOn bpen kon jung-wùt ____krúp?

       Thai   jung-wùt na-korn pa-nom kà

   c Foreigner   bprai-sa-nee yòo glai ____krúp?

       Thai   mâi glai krúp

   d Foreigner   hôrng náhm yòo ____krúp?

       Thai   yòo kûng bon kà

2 Read the following conversation and answer the questions.

Foreigner	kŏr-tôht krúp tăir-o née mee bprai-sa-nee mái?
Thai	mee kà yòo têe nôhn glâi glâi ta-nah-kahn
	kŏr-tôht kOOn bpen kon châht a-rai ká?
Foreigner	pŏm bpen kon jeen krúp chêu: lĭn krúp
	kŏr-tôht kOOn chêu: a-rai krúp?
Thai	chêu: lék kà
Foreigner	kOOn lék bpen kon grOOng-tâyp châi mái krúp?
Thai	mâi châi kà bpen kon ee-săhn kà
Foreigner	jung-wùt a-rai krúp?
Thai	jung-wùt na-korn pa-nom kà

   a Is the foreigner a male or female?

   b Is the Thai a male or female?

   c What is the foreigner looking for?

   d Where is it?

   e What nationality is the foreigner?

   f What is the foreigner's name?

   g What is the Thai's name?

   h Which province does the Thai come from?

   i What part of Thailand is that province in?

3 How would you read the following words?

วัน	ขอ	ดู	มี	ไหน
งาน	อัน	ไป	หมอ	จาน
หา	ดำ	ใน	กิน	โมง

4 How would you read the following phrases?

a ไปลอนดอน

b ไปหาหมอ

c ไปดูหนัง

mee pêe nórng mái?

*Do you have any
brothers and sisters?*

In this unit you will learn how to:
▶ *talk about family members.*
▶ *ask how many? questions.*
▶ *ask whether or not something has happened.*
▶ *recognize more common low class consonants.*
▶ *read some simple statements about people.*

CEFR: *(A1) Can ask for and provide personal information; can describe
his/her family.*

Families

There are many more kin terms in Thai than in English, because there
are different words for relatives on the mother's side and on the father's
side. Some kin terms convey information about age and seniority,
but not gender.

It is common in Thai small talk to ask a relative stranger, **mee pêe nórng
mái?** (*Have you got any brothers and sisters?*). Think how long it would
take most Northern Europeans before they would consider asking such
a question in their own language; no wonder they come back from
Thailand, amazed at the friendliness of Thai people. The question literally
asks whether you have any *older siblings* (**pêe**) and *younger siblings*
(**nórng**). The question focuses on age and seniority and makes no
reference to gender. Indeed, you may hear someone refer to a member
of their family as **pêe** and you will not know whether they are talking
about an older brother or older sister. However, when it is necessary to be
specific, or avoid ambiguity, the word **chai:** (*male*) or **săo:** (*female*) is
added after **pêe** or **nórng**.

How would you say *yes* if a Thai asked you, **mee pêe nórng mái?** (Don't
forget the polite particle!) And if you're an only child, how will you reply?

Vocabulary builder

04.01 **Listen to the audio and repeat each word after the speaker. Try to imitate the speaker as closely as you can.**

TALKING ABOUT FAMILIES

พี่น้อง	pêe nórng	*brothers and sisters*
น้องชาย	nórng chai	*younger brother*
ทำงาน	tum ngahn	*to work*
อีก	èek	*another; again*
นักหนังสือพิมพ์	núk núng-sěu pim	*journalist*
นักศึกษา	núk sèuk-sǎh	*student*
กี่	gèe	*how many?*
พี่สาว	pêe sǎo:	*older sister*
น้องสาว	nórng sǎo:	*younger sister*
แต่งงาน	dtàirng ngahn	*to get married*
… แล้วหรือยัง	… láir-o réu yung?	*… yet?*
แฟน	fairn	*boyfriend, girlfriend; partner; spouse*
แต่	dtàir	*but*
ลูก	lôok	*child*
ลูกชาย	lôok chai:	*son*
ลูกสาว	lôok sǎo:	*daughter*
อายุ	ah-yÓO	*age*
เท่าไหร่	tâo-rài?	*how much?*
สิบสาม	sìp sǎhm	*13*
เจ็ด	jèt	*seven*
ขวบ	kòo-up	*years old (up to the age of about ten)*

NEW EXPRESSIONS

มีพี่น้องไหม	mee pêe nórng mái ?	Do you have any brothers and sisters?
ทำงานอะไร	tum ngahn a-rai?	What (job) do they do?
มีพี่น้องกี่คน	mee pêe nórng gèe kon?	How many brothers and sisters do you have?
แต่งงาน(แล้ว)หรือยัง	dtàirng ngahn (láir-o) réu yung?	Are they married?
มีลูก(แล้ว)หรือยัง	mee lôok (láir-o) réu yung?	Do they have any children?
อายุเท่าไหร่	ah-yÓO tâo-rài?	How old are you?
อายุสิบสาม	ah-yÓO sìp sǎhm	13 years old
อายุเจ็ดขวบ	ah-yÓO jèt kòo-up	seven years old

Conversations

 04.02 *Somjit asks Steve about his family.*

1 Does Steve have any brothers and sisters?

Somjit	คุณสตีฟมีพี่น้องไหมคะ	kOOn Sa-dteef mee pêe nórng mái ká?
Steve	มีครับ	mee krúp
	มีน้องชายสองคนครับ	mee nórng chai sǒrng kon krúp
Somjit	ทำงานอะไรคะ	tum ngahn a-rai ká?
Steve	คนหนึ่งเป็นนักหนังสือพิมพ์	kon nèung bpen núk núng-sěu pim
	อีกคนหนึ่งไม่ทำงาน	èek kon nèung mâi tum ngahn
	เป็นนักศึกษา	bpen núk sèuk-săh

2 Read and listen to the conversation again and answer these questions.

   a How many brothers and sisters does Steve have?
   b Are they older or younger than him?
   c What gender are they?
   d What job do they do?

3 How many brothers and sisters does Wanpen have?

Sue	คุณวันเพ็ญมีพี่น้องกี่คนคะ	kOOn Wun-pen mee pêe nórng gèe kon ká?
Wanpen	สองคนค่ะ	sŏrng kon kà
	มีพี่สาวคนหนึ่ง	mee pêe săo: kon nèung
	น้องสาวคนหนึ่ง	nórng săo: kon nèung
Sue	แต่งงานแล้วหรือยังคะ	dtàirng ngahn láir-o réu yung ká?
Wanpen	พี่สาวแต่งงานแล้ว	pêe săo: dtàirng ngahn láir-o
	น้องสาวมีแฟนแล้ว	nórng săo: mee fairn láir-o
	แต่ยังไม่แต่งงาน	dtàir yung mâi dtàirng ngahn
Sue	พี่สาวมีลูกแล้วหรือยังคะ	pêe săo: mee lôok láir-o réu yung ká?
Wanpen	มีแล้ว	mee láir-o
	มีลูกชายสองคน	mee lôok chai sŏrng kon

4 Read and listen to the conversation again and answer the following questions

    a Is Wanpen the eldest, the middle or youngest child in her family?
    b Which sister is married?
    c How many children does the married sister have?
    d Are the children boys or girls?

> **LANGUAGE TIP**
>
> The word **lôok** (*child, children*) means *children* in the sense of *offspring*. You can use it in sentences like, *How many children has she got?* and *His children are a menace!*, but if you want to talk about children as an age category, such as *Children nowadays have a tough time*, or *Children must be accompanied by an adult*, you have to use **dèk** (*child, children*) instead.

5   Is Somchai's brother married?

Wanpen	พี่ชายมีแฟนหรือยังคะ	pêe chai: mee fairn réu yung ká?
Somchai	มีแล้วครับ	mee láir-o krúp
	แต่งงานแล้ว มีลูก	dtàirng ngahn láir-o mee lôok
Wanpen	มีลูกกี่คนคะ	mee lôok gèe kon ká?
Somchai	มีสองคนครับ	mee sŏrng kon krúp
	ลูกชายคนหนึ่ง	lôok chai: kon nèung
	ลูกสาวคนหนึ่ง	lôok sǎo: kon nèung
Wanpen	อายุเท่าไหร่คะ	ah-yÓO tâo-rài ká?
Somchai	ลูกชายอายุสิบสาม	lôok chai: ah-yÓO sìp sǎhm
	ลูกสาวอายุเจ็ดขวบ	lôok sǎo: ah-yÓO jèt kòo-up

6   Read and listen to the conversation again and then answer these questions.

   a   Is Somchai's brother older or younger than him?
   b   How many children does Somchai's brother have?
   c   What gender are the children?
   d   How old are they?

Language discovery

 04.05 Here are some of the words you may need in order to be able to talk about your family members. The words **chai:** (*male*) and **săo:** (*female*), are used to distinguish the gender of *older* (**pêe**) and *younger* (**nórng**) siblings and also *children* (**lôok**).

พี่น้อง	**pêe nórng**	*brothers and sisters*
พี่ชาย	**pêe chai:**	*older brother*
พี่สาว	~~**pêe săo:**~~	*older sister*
น้องชาย	**nórng chai:**	*younger brother*
น้องสาว	**nórng săo:**	*younger sister*
ลูกชาย	**lôok chai:**	*son*
ลูกสาว	**lôok săo:**	*daughter*
พ่อ	**pôr**	*father*
แม่	**mâir**	*mother*

> **LANGUAGE TIP**
>
> To say *my father*, *your mother*, *his sister* and so on, use the kin term followed by the pronoun: **pôr pŏm** (literally, *father-I*), **mâir kOOn** (*mother-you*), **nórng săo: káo** (*sister-he*).

How much can you say about your family? Pretend you are explaining who the people are in a family snapshot. Try to say as much as you can about each person. Here is an example to help you.

pôr pŏm bpen kon lorn-dorn

mâir pŏm bpen kon tai

pŏm mee nórng săo: kon nèung chêu: Kate.

Kate dtàirng ngahn láir-o mee lôok sŏrng kon,

lôok chai: kon nèung, lôok săo: kon nèung.

lôok chai: ah-yÓO hâh kòo-up

lôok săo: ah-yÓO săhm kòo-up.

1 NOUNS, NUMBERS AND CLASSIFIERS

Thai nouns do not have separate forms for singular and plural. Usually the context is sufficient to know whether the noun is singular or plural. But when it is necessary to be specific, Thai uses various 'pluralizer' words or numbers. Whenever nouns and numbers are combined, in phrases like *three children*, Thai uses an additional word, caller a classifier, in the pattern, NOUN + NUMBER + CLASSIFIER. In this unit we meet the word **kon** (*person*) again, but this time it is acting as a classifier for human beings:

มีน้องชายสองคน   **mee nórng chai: sŏrng kon**
I have two younger brothers.
(literally: *have-younger brother-two-person*)

มีลูกชายสองคน   **mee lôok chai: sŏrng kon**
He has two sons.

nèung (*one*) can occur either before the classifier (like other number words), or after the classifier, in which case it can be translated as *a/an* rather than *one*:

มีพี่สาวคนหนึ่ง   **mee pêe sǎo: kon nèung**
I have an older sister.

2 HOW MANY?

How many? questions are formed by the pattern VERB + NOUN + **gèe** + CLASSIFIER:

มีพี่น้องกี่คน   **mee pêe nórng gèe kon?**
How many brothers and sisters do you have?

The answer normally takes the form (VERB) + NUMBER + CLASSIFIER:

(มี)สองคน   **(mee) sŏrng kon**   *(I have) two.*

3 ... (láir-o) réu yung? QUESTIONS

Questions that end in **... (láir-o) réu yung?** ask whether something has happened yet or not. The word **láir-o** (*already*) is often omitted and the question shortened to **... réu yung?** A *yes* answer to **a ... (láir-o) réu yung?** question is VERB + **láir-o**; a *no* answer is **yung**:

แต่งงานแล้วหรือยัง
Is she married?

แต่งงานแล้ว
Yes.

ยัง
No.

มีแฟนหรือยัง
Does he have a girlfriend?

มีแล้ว
Yes.

ยัง
No.

4 AGE

To ask how old someone is, use **ah-yÓO** (*age*) + **tâo-rài?** (*how much?*). There are two patterns for stating someone's age. For children up to the age of about ten, use **ah-yÓO** (*age*) + NUMBER + **kòo-up** (*years old*); for people older than that, the pattern is **ah-yÓO** (*age*) + NUMBER + **bpee** (*year*), although **bpee** is often omitted.

อายุเท่าไหร่
How old are they?

ลูกชายอายุสิบสาม
My son is 13.

ลูกสาวอายุเจ็ดขวบ
My daughter is seven.

🔓 Practice

1. **How would you answer if someone asked you the following:**
   a mee pêe nórng mái?
   b mee fairn réu yung?
   c dtàirng ngahn láir-o réu yung?

2. **Fill in the gaps in the dialogue.**

Wanpen		kOOn mee pêe nórng mái ká?
Peter	a	_____ krúp
Wanpen		mee pêe nórng gèe kon ká?
Peter	b	sŏrng _____
	c	pêe chai: _____
	d	nórng chai: _____
Wanpen	e	dtàirng ngahn _____ ká?
Peter		pêe chai: dtàirng ngahn láir-o krúp
	f	dtàir nórng chai: _____

3. **How would you ask:**
   a Excuse me, are you married?
   b Do you have any children?
   c How old are your children?

4. **How would you say the following?**
   a I have one older brother and one younger sister.
   b I have two younger brothers.
   c I have two older sisters and one younger sister.
   d I don't have any brothers and sisters.

Pronunciation

04.06 **Listen to the audio and repeat after the speaker.**

yung réu yung?	láir-o réu yung?	mee fairn láir-o réu yung?
yung réu yung?	láir-o réu yung?	dtàirng ngahn láir-o réu yung?
yung réu yung?	láir-o réu yung?	mee lôok láir-o réu yung?

Go further

Both **pêe** (*older sibling*) and **nórng** (*younger sibling*) are also used as pronouns. They create a sense of both intimacy and hierarchy between speakers. **pêe** has an especially wide range of usage. An older person might use **pêe** to mean *I* (instead of the more formal **pǒm/di-chún**) when talking to a younger friend. A younger person may use **pêe** to mean *you* (instead of the more formal **kOOn**) when talking to an older friend or work colleague, as may wives and girlfriends when addressing their partners.

nórng is often used in restaurants to summon a waiter or waitress, although this is only appropriate if the person is visibly younger.

Reading and writing

 04.07 In this unit we continue to add more consonants and vowels and meet one or two irregularities, where a symbol changes its pronunciation under certain specific circumstances. Don't worry if you can't absorb all the information at once. Maintain an up-to-date crib sheet of letters and spelling rules and keep it close at hand until you feel ready to dispense with it.

CONSONANTS

The new consonants in this unit are all low class consonants, like those in Unit 1.

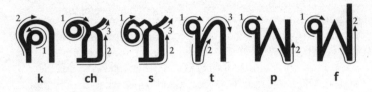

| k | ch | s | t | p | f |

VOWELS

| -eu | -eu: | -ay | -air |
| (short vowel) | (long vowel) | (long vowel) | (long vowel) |

The symbol ◌ื is unusual in that if there is no final consonant (i.e. the word ends with an **-eu** sound) the zero consonant symbol must be added:

with final consonant

| คืน | ลืม | ยืน |
| keu:n | leu:m | yeu:n |

no final consonant

| คือ | ลือ | มือ |
| keu: | leu: | meu: |

The symbol เ- changes from an **-ay** sound to **er-ee** when it occurs with the consonant ย at the end of the word:

เ-

| เกม | เบน | เลน |
| gaym | bayn | layn |

เ-ย

| เลย | เคย | เนย |
| ler-ee | ker-ee | ner-ee |

VOWEL SHORTENER SYMBOL

When the symbol ◌ͬ which is identical to the number eight appears above a consonant and in conjunction with the vowel symbols เ- and, less commonly แ-, the vowels change from long vowels to short vowels. The symbol ◌ͬ also occurs above the letter ก with no accompanying written vowel; this word is pronounced **gôr.**

เป็น	เย็น	ก็
bpen	**yen**	**gôr**

The following words all have a mid tone. Practise reading them out loud with the Romanized transcription covered up. Listen to them on the audio to check your pronunciation and then write them out several times.

คำ	ชาย	ชาม	ซอย
kum	**chai:**	**chahm**	**soi:**

ทำ	ทาง	แพง	แดง
tum	**tahng**	**pairng**	**dairng**

ดึง	คืน	เคย	เป็น
deung	**keu:n**	**ker-ee**	**bpen**

WORDS WITH NO VOWEL SYMBOL (I)

When a word consists of two consonant symbols with no written vowel symbol, a short **-o** vowel must be supplied. Cover the Romanized transcription and listen to the following words:

คน	ผม	งง	สน	ชน	ฝน
kon	**pǒm**	**ngong**	**sǒn**	**chon**	**fǒn**

？ Test yourself

04.08 **Listen to the audio and check your answers in the Answer Key.**

1 **How would you ask the following?**
   a Do you have any brothers and sisters?
   b How many brothers and sisters do you have?
   c How old are you?

2 **How would you say the following?**
   a He has three brothers and sisters.
   b I have two older sisters and one younger brother.
   c I don't have any brothers and sisters.

3 **How would you ask if someone …**
   a is married?
   b has any children?
   c has eaten (**gin** *to eat*) yet?
   d has gone (**bpai** *to go*) yet?

4 **What pronoun has been deliberately omitted at the beginning of the sentence …**
   a … when Steve says, **mee nórng chai sŏrng kon krúp** (Conversation 1)
   b … when Somjit asks, **tum ngahn a-rai ká?** (Conversation 1)
   c … when Sue asks, **dtàirng ngahn láir-o réu yung ká?** (Conversation 2)
   d … when Wanpen asks, **mee lôok gèe kon ká?** (Conversation 3)

5 **How would you read these common words:**
   a เป็น to be
   b คน person
   c ทำ to do
   d ผม I (male)
   e แพง expensive
   f ชาย male

6 **Read these three sentences and then answer the questions.**

หลิงเป็นคนจีน สมชายเป็นคนอีสาน ซูเป็นหมอ

   a What nationality is Ling? What tone is her name pronounced with?
   b What part of Thailand does Somchai come from?
   c What is Sue's occupation? (If you're not sure, you can find the answer in Test yourself Q4 in the last unit.)

SELF CHECK

	I CAN…
○	…talk about family members.
○	…ask *how many?* questions.
○	…ask whether or not something has happened.
○	…recognize more common low class consonants.
○	…read some simple statements about people.

5 chôrp tahn ah-hăhn tai mái?

Do you like eating Thai food?

In this unit you will learn how to:
- ▶ *respond appropriately to simple questions about food and eating.*
- ▶ *order simple food.*
- ▶ *read words with tone marks.*
- ▶ *write answers in Thai script to simple questions about members of the family.*

CEFR: *(A1) Can respond to typical questions about food and eating; can order a meal.*

Eating

Most Thais take a great interest in and spend a lot of time talking about food and eating. Asking someone whether they have eaten yet – **tahn kâo: réu yung?** or **gin kâo: réu yung?** – is even widely used as an informal greeting. Whether it is true or not, most people respond with **tahn láir-o** or **gin láir-o**. Two basic words to know when talking about Thai food are **a-ròy** (*tasty*) and **pèt** (*spicy*). They occur in standard questions Thais will ask foreigners, such as **ah-hăhn** (*food*) **tai a-ròy mái?** and **ah-hăhn tai pèt mái?** These are formulaic small talk questions; you are supposed to answer *yes*, so curb all inclinations to establish your unique identity with a clever answer and just do what is expected of you.

So, what would your answers to these questions be (and don't forget the polite particle so that you don't sound abrupt!)?

Vocabulary builder

FOOD

ทาน	tahn	*to eat (formal)*
กิน	gin	*to eat (informal)*
สั่ง	sùng	*to order*
ชอบ	chôrp	*to like*
อาหาร	ah-hăhn	*food*
ไทย	tai	*Thai*
อยากจะ ...	yàhk ja ...	*would like to ...*
เผ็ด	pèt	*spicy*
... เป็นไหม	... bpen mái?	*can you ...?*
อร่อย	a-ròy	*tasty*
ขนม	ka-nŏm	*dessert*
อิ่ม	ìm	*to be full up*
เอา	ao	*to want*
ข้าว	kâo:	*rice*
ข้าวผัด	kâo: pùt	*fried rice*
กุ้ง	gÔOng	*shrimp*
กาแฟเย็น	gah-fair yen	*iced coffee*

NEW EXPRESSIONS

ทาน/กินข้าวหรือยัง	tahn/gin kâo: réu yung?	*Have you eaten yet?*
สั่งหรือยัง	sùng réu yung?	*Have you ordered yet?*
ชอบทานอาหารไทยไหม	chôrp tahn ah-hăhn tai mái?	*Do you like eating Thai food?*
อยากจะทานอะไรบ้าง	yàhk ja tahn a-rai bâhng?	*What would you like to eat?*
อะไรก็ได้	a-rai gôr dâi	*Anything (you like/ will do)*
ทานอาหารเผ็ดเป็นไหม	tahn ah-hăhn pèt bpen mái?	*Can you eat spicy food?*
อิ่มแล้ว	ìm láir-o	*I'm full up*
น้อง	nórng!	*Waiter/Waitress!*
เช็คบิลด้วย	chék bin dôo-ay	*Can I have the bill, please?*
เอาน้ำอะไร	ao náhm a-rai?	*What do you want to drink?*

Conversations

1 Can Steve eat spicy food?

Waiter	สั่งหรือยังครับ	sùng réu yung krúp?
Somjit	ยังค่ะ	yung kà
	คุณสตีฟชอบทาน	kOOn Sa-dteef chôrp tahn
	อาหารไทยไหมคะ	ah-hăhn tai mái ká?
Steve	ชอบครับ	chôrp krúp
Somjit	อยากจะทานอะไรคะ	yàhk ja tahn a-rai ká?
Steve	อะไรก็ได้ครับ	a-rai gôr dâi krúp
Somjit	ทานอาหารเผ็ดเป็นไหม	tahn ah-hăhn pèt bpen mái?
Steve	เป็นครับ	bpen krúp

2 Read and listen to the conversation again and answer these questions

a How does Somjit say *no* when the waiter asks if she has ordered yet?

b Does Steve like Thai food?

c What would Steve like to eat?

d Find the word for *Can you …?* when Somjit asks, *Can you eat spicy food?*

e How does Steve say *yes* to Somjit's question about eating spicy food?

3 Why doesn't Steve want dessert?

Somjit	อาหารอร่อยไหมคะ	ah-hăhn a-ròy mái ká?
Steve	อร่อยครับ อร่อยมาก	a-ròy krúp. a-ròy mâhk
Somjit	ทานขนมไหม	tahn ka-nŏm mái?
Steve	ไม่ทานครับ	mâi tahn krúp
	อิ่มแล้วครับ	ìm láir-o krúp
Somjit	น้องคะ	nórng ká!
	เช็คบิลด้วยค่ะ	chék bin dôo-ay kà

4 Read and listen to the conversation again and answer these questions.

    a How does Steve say that the food is very tasty?

    b How does Steve say, *I'm full up?*

    c How does Somjit address the waitress?

    d How does she call for the bill?

> **LANGUAGE TIP**
>
> If the waiter or waitress is the same age as you, or older, you can use **kOOn** (*you!*) +
> polite particle: **kOOn krúp!** or **kOOn ká!**
>
> **bin** in **chék bin dôo-ay** is the English word *bill*. Thai words don't end in an **l** sound
> and when Thais pronounce English words with a final **l**, they normally replace it with
> an **n** sound.

 05.04 *Sue is ordering food.*

5 What food does Sue order?

Waitress	เอาอะไรคะ	ao a-rai ká?
Sue	มีข้าวผัดไหมคะ	mee kâo: pùt mái ká?
Waitress	มีค่ะ	mee kà
Sue	เอาข้าวผัดกุ้งค่ะ	ao kâo: pùt gÔOng kà
Waitress	ค่ะ	kà
	แล้วเอาน้ำอะไรคะ	láir-o ao náhm a-rai ká?
Sue	เอากาแฟเย็นค่ะ	ao gah-fair yen kà

6 Read and listen to the conversation again and answer these questions.

    a What kind of fried rice does Sue want?

    b How does the waitress say, *yes/right/OK*, in response to Sue's order?

    c What does she order to drink?

    d What word do the waitress and Sue use for *want/would like?*

💡 Language discovery

1 LIKE AND WOULD LIKE TO …

Be careful not to confuse **chôrp** (*to like*) and **yàhk ja …** (*would like to, want to …*) and **ao** (*to want*). **chôrp** can be followed by either a verb or a noun, **yàhk ja …** is followed by a verb and **ao** is followed by a noun:

chôrp tahn ah-hăhn tai mái?

ชอบทานอาหารไทยไหม

Do you like eating Thai food?

chôrp ah-hăhn tai mái?

ชอบอาหารไทยไหม

Do you like Thai food?

yàhk ja tahn a-rai?

อยากจะทานอะไร

What would you like to eat?

ao kâo: pùt gÔOng

เอาข้าวผัดกุ้ง

I want/I'd like shrimp fried rice.

When **yàhk ja …** is used in questions with **mái?** (Would you like to …?), a *yes* answer is **yàhk** (without **ja**) and a *no* answer is **mâi yàhk:**.

yàhk ja tahn ah-hăhn tai mái?	**yàhk**	**mâi yàhk**

อยากจะทานอาหารไทยไหม   อยาก   ไม่อยาก

Would you like to eat Thai food?   *Yes.*   *No.*

2 TO EAT

tahn and **gin** both mean *to eat*. As a foreign learner of Thai you need to know both. **tahn** is more formal than **gin**, but it is also a way of showing politeness and respect towards the person you are talking to. Don't think, *I'm an informal kinda guy, with limited memory space – I'll forget about* **tahn** *and just use* **gin** *'cos it sounds more like my kinda word!* If you adopt this strategy, you'll risk sounding badly inappropriate in certain situations. Listen out for these two words when you hear Thais talking among themselves and see how their choices match your perception of the situation and the relationship between the speakers.

3 a-rai gôr dâi

a-rai gôr dâi (*anything you like*) is a valuable way of expressing amenability to someone else's suggestion. If a Thai takes you out for a meal, he or she is, of course, duty-bound to ask you what you want to eat; but you're not duty-bound to be specific, and your host will probably be only too delighted if you relinquish all responsibility for ordering.

... gôr dâi can also be used after a number of other question words. For example, **têe-năi gôr dâi** means *anywhere you like*, and **krai** (*who?*) **gôr dâi** means *anyone you like*.

4 VERB + bpen

In Unit 2 you met the pattern, **bpen** (*is/are*) + NOUN (e.g. **bpen kon tai**). In this unit **bpen** occurs in the pattern, VERB + **bpen**, and means *to know how to do something* or *can*. Questions that take the form, VERB + **bpen mái?** (*Can you ...?*), are answered either **bpen** (*yes*) or **mâi bpen** (*no*):

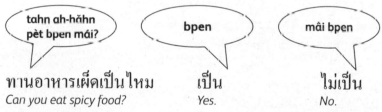

ทานอาหารเผ็ดเป็นไหม
Can you eat spicy food?

เป็น
Yes.

ไม่เป็น
No.

If you want to say you can't do something, the negative word **mâi** goes immediately before bpen:

สั่งอาหารไทยไม่เป็น **sùng ah-hăhn tai mâi bpen** *I can't order Thai food.*

5 láir-o

We've met **láir-o** in the pattern VERB + **láir-o** as a *yes* answer to a **... réu yung** question (Unit 4). It is used after verbs to indicate that the action of the verb has been completed, and after adjectives to show that a state of the adjective has been reached:

กินแล้ว   **gin láir-o**   *I've eaten.*

อิ่มแล้ว   **ìm láir-o**   *I'm full.*

In spoken Thai, it can occur at the beginning of a sentence as a way of changing the focus of the conversation:

แล้วเอาน้ำอะไร   **láir-o ao náhm a-rai?**   *And what would you like to drink?*
(i.e. I've noted what you want to eat, now let's change the focus to drinks.)

Practice

1 **How would you say *no* to the following questions?**
   a tahn kâo: réu yung ká?
   b tahn ah-hǎhn pèt bpen mái ká?
   c yàhk ja gin ah-hǎhn tai mái ká?
   d ìm láir-o châi mái ká?

2 **How would you say the following?**
   a I'd like to eat Thai food.
   b Wanpen would like to eat spicy food.
   c Sue likes eating fried rice.
   d Sue wants shrimp fried rice.

3 **Use the prompts to respond to the Thai person's questions.**

Thai		kOOn yàhk ja gin a-rai krúp?
You	a	(Say, *Anything you like.*)
Thai		yàhk ja gin têe-nǎi krúp?
You	b	(Say, *Anywhere you like.*)

 Pronunciation

05.05 **Listen to the audio and repeat after the speaker, paying careful attention to the tones.**

krúp	dâi krúp	gôr dâi krúp	a-rai gôr dâi krúp
kà	dâi kà	gôr dâi kà	a-rai gôr dâi kà
krúp	dâi krúp	gôr dâi krúp	têe-nǎi gôr dâi krúp
kà	dâi kà	gôr dâi kà	têe-nǎi gôr dâi kà

Reading and writing

So far we have seen how the class of the initial consonant plays a role in determining the tone of a word. In this lesson we learn how tone marks are used to indicate the pitch of a word. When you come to the Test Yourself section you will find that you can now read the words that you learned in the last unit for older and younger brothers and sisters.

TONE MARKS

Tone marks are written above the initial consonant. If the initial consonant already has a vowel above it, then the tone mark is written above that vowel.

The two most common tone marks are **mái àyk** – which looks like a number 1 – and **mái toh** – which, with a bit of imagination, looks like a number 2, albeit with an elongated tail. It would make obvious sense if each tone mark represented one tone. Unfortunately for the learner, this is not the case. Due to changes in the language that have taken place over hundreds of years, words with **mái àyk** are pronounced with either a falling tone or a low tone, while words written with **mái toh** have either a high tone or a falling tone. The determining factor is the class of the initial consonant. If **mái àyk** occurs above a low class initial consonant, the tone of the word will be falling; if the initial consonant is either mid class or high class, then the tone is low.

1 05.06 **Cover up the Romanized transcription and focus on the Thai script as you listen to the following words:**

Low class	ไม่	ใช่	ที่	พี่
	mâi	**châi**	**têe**	**pêe**
Mid class	ไก่	บ่าย	ต่อ	อิ่ม
	gài	**bài:**	**dtòr**	**ìm**
High class	ไข่	สี่	ห่อ	สั่ง
	kài	**sèe**	**hòr**	**sùng**

If **mái toh** occurs above a low class initial consonant, the tone of the word will be high; if the initial consonant is either mid class or high class, then the tone is falling:

 2 05.07 **Again, cover up the Romanized transcription and focus on the Thai script as you listen to these words:**

Low class	แล้ว	น้อง	ย้าย	นั้น
	láir-o	nórng	yái:	nún

Mid class	บ้าน	ต้อง	ได้	กุ้ง
	bâhn	dtôrng	dâi	gÔOng

High class	ข้าว	ถ้า	ห้อง	ให้
	kâo:	tâh	hôrng	hâi

3 Practise writing the words out in Thai script and saying each one out loud as you do so.

There are two further tone marks which are much less common than **mái àyk** and **mái toh**. **mái dtree** is identical to the Thai number 7; it always produces a high tone. **mái jùt-dta-wah** is a cross; it always produces a rising tone.

SUMMARY OF TONE MARK RULES

Initial consonant class	mái àyk ᐟ ▬	mái toh ᵛ ▬	mái dtree ᧡ ▬	mái jùt-dta-wah + ▬
Low class	**Falling tone**	**High tone**	**High tone**	**Rising tone**
Mid class	**Low tone**	**Falling tone**	**High tone**	**Rising tone**
High class	**Low tone**	**Falling tone**	**High tone**	**Rising tone**

> **LANGUAGE TIP**
> Make a copy of this table and keep it close at hand when you are reading Thai words; gradually you will find you absorb the rules and become less dependent on it.

Test yourself

Listen to the audio and check your answers in the Answer Key.

1 How would you say *yes* **to the following questions:**
   a   chôrp tahn ah-hăhn tai mái krúp?
   b   tahn ah-hăhn pèt bpen mái krúp?
   c   ah-hăhn tai a-ròy châi mái krúp?
   d   ìm réu yung krúp?

2 How would you say the following?
   a   He would like to eat fried rice.
   b   He wouldn't like to eat spicy food.
   c   Sue likes eating Thai food.
   d   Sue doesn't like eating Chinese food.

3 How would you translate the following?
   a   ao a-rai ká?   c   a-ròy mái ká?
   b   tahn ka-nŏm mái ká?   d   ìm réu yung ká?

4 Here are some more common words. How would you read them?

   a   สั่ง   to order   d   ได้   can, to be able to

   b   อิ่ม   full (after eating)   e   แล้ว   already

   c   ไม่ใช่   no, not   f   ข้าว   rice

5 Read this short statement about Somchai and then answer the questions.

สมชาย มีพี่น้องห้าคน มีพี่ชายสองคน น้องสาวสามคน

   a   How many brothers and sisters does Somchai have?
   b   Are his brothers older or younger than him?
   c   How many sisters does he have?

6 Read the following questions (which are addressed to you) and write the answer, *yes* **or** *no*, **in Thai script.**

   a   มีพี่น้องไหม   c   มีพี่สาวไหม   e   มีน้องสาวไหม
   b   มีพี่ชายไหม   d   มีน้องชายไหม

SELF CHECK

	I CAN...
○	...respond appropriately to simple questions about food and eating.
○	...order simple food.
○	...read words with tone marks.
○	...write answers in Thai script to simple questions about members of the family.

6 nêe tâo-rài?

How much is this?

In this unit you will learn how to:
▶ ask the price of things.
▶ ask to look at or try on something.
▶ shop for items by colour.
▶ read 'dead' syllables.

CEFR: *(A1) Can ask the price and ask to look at something before making a purchase.*

◉ Shopping

From traditional markets to ultra-modern, multi-storeyed shopping arcades, Thai cities in general, and Bangkok especially, offer a rich variety of shopping facilities. While shops operate on fixed prices, owners may sometimes offer a small discount in order to seal the deal. Lively haggling, once a common sight in early morning fresh food markets, has all but disappeared, although it is still useful when buying at roadside stalls, especially those that aim to attract foreign customers. To do this, you simply state a price lower than that quoted, followed by **dâi mái?** (*can you?*). When asking the price of something, you can get by quite comfortably by simply pointing at something and saying, **tâo-rài?** (*how much?*). More specific questions, like, *How much is this shirt?* or *How much is that pair of shoes?*, are more linguistically demanding, but are worth mastering because they offer you the opportunity to sound more impressive in your spoken Thai.

Vocabulary builder

 06.01 **Listen to the audio and repeat each word after the speaker. Try to imitate the speaker as closely as you can, and try to think about the tone that you are hearing as you listen.**

SHOPPING

นี่	nêe	this
ร้อย	róy	a hundred
หกร้อย	hòk róy	six hundred
บาท	bàht	baht (unit of Thai currency)
ขอ	kŏr	to ask for something/to do something
ขอ ... หน่อย	kŏr ... nòy	Please could I ...?
ดู	doo	to look at
ได้	dâi	to be able; can
.., ได้ไหม	... dâi măi?	Can I/you/he/she, etc. ...?
ห้าร้อย	hâh róy	five hundred
เสื้อ	sêu-a	shirt, blouse, top
ตัว	dtoo-a	classifier for shirts
นั้น	nún	that
สี	sĕe	colour
สีแดง	sĕe dairng	red
ลอง	lorng	to try on/out something
ดี	dee	good
สวย	sŏo-ay	pretty, beautiful
อย่างไร	yung-ngai?	how?
รองเท้า	rorng táo:	shoe(s)
คู่	kôo	pair
นี้	née	this
ใส่	sài	to wear, put on
เบอร์	ber	size

NEW EXPRESSIONS

นี่เท่าไหร่	nêe tâo-rài?	*How much is this?*
ขอดูหน่อยได้ไหม	kŏr doo nòy dâi mái?	*Can I have a look, please?*
ขอลองดูหน่อยได้ไหม	kŏr lorng doo nòy dâi mái?	*Can I try it on, please?*
เป็นอย่างไร	bpen yung-ngai?	*How is it?*
ใส่เบอร์อะไร	sài ber a-rai?	*What size do you take?*
ลองเบอร์สิบได้ไหม	lorng ber sìp dâi mái?	*Can I try size 10?*

Conversations

 06.02 *Sue is looking at bags on a market stall.*

1 How much does the vendor say the bag costs?

Sue	นี่เท่าไหร่คะ	nêe tâo-rài ká?
Vendor	หกร้อยบาทครับ	hòk róy bàht krúp
Sue	เท่าไหร่นะ	tâo-rài ná?
Vendor	หกร้อยบาทครับ	hòk róy bàht krúp
Sue	ขอดูหน่อยได้ไหม	kŏr doo nòy dâi mái?
Vendor	ได้ครับ	dâi krúp
Sue	ห้าร้อยได้ไหมคะ	hâh róy dâi mái ká?
Vendor	ได้ครับ	dâi krúp

2 **Read and listen to the conversation again and answer these questions:**

  a How does Sue ask the vendor to repeat the price?

  b How does Sue ask to have a look at the bag?

  c How does the vendor say yes?

  d What price does the vendor agree to accept?

> **LANGUAGE TIP**
> Numbers from 200–900 are formed in a regular way; see Appendix.

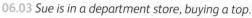 06.03 *Sue is in a department store, buying a top.*

3 **What colour of top does Sue want?**

Sue	เสื้อตัวนั้นเท่าไหร่คะ	sêu-a dtoo-a nún tâo-rài ká?
Salesgirl	แปดร้อยบาทค่ะ	bpàirt róy bàht kà
	ชอบสีอะไรคะ	chôrp sěe a-rai ká?
Sue	ชอบสีแดงค่ะ	chôrp sée dairng kà
	ขอลองดูหน่อยได้ไหม	kǒr lorng doo nòy dâi mái?
Salesgirl	ได้ค่ะ	dâi kà
	สีแดงสวยนะคะ	sěe dairng sǒo-ay ná ká
	เป็นอย่างไรคะ	bpen yung-ngai ká?
Sue	ดีค่ะ สวยมาก	dee kù, sǒo-ay mâhk

4 **Read and listen to the conversation again and answer these questions:**

  a How much does the top cost?

  b How does Sue ask to try it on?

  c What does Sue think of the top?

> **LANGUAGE TIP**
> The **ná** in the Salesgirl's **sǒo-ay ná ká** is seeking agreement; we could translate her words as *Red is pretty, isn't it?*

5 Do the shoes fit?

Steve	รองเท้าคู่นี้เท่าไหร่ครับ	rorng táo: kôo née tâo-rài krúp?
Sales girl	เก้าร้อยบาทค่ะ	gâo: róy bàht kà
	ลองดูไหมคะ	lorng doo mái ká?
Steve	ลองครับ	lorng krúp
Sales girl	ใส่เบอร์อะไรคะ	sài ber a-rai ká?
Steve	เบอร์เก้าครับ	ber gâo: krúp
Sales girl	เป็นอย่างไรคะ	bpen yung-ngai ká?
	ใส่ได้ไหม	sài dâi mái?
Steve	ไม่ได้ครับ	mâi dâi krúp
	ขอลองเบอร์สิบได้ไหม	kŏr lorng ber sìp dâi mái?

> **LANGUAGE TIP**
>
> **sài dâi mái?** literally means, *Can you wear it?* but it is the normal way of asking, *Does it fit?* The word **ber** (*size*) is taken from the English *number*.

6 Read and listen to the conversation again and answer these questions:

a How much do the shoes cost?

b What size does Steve normally take?

c What size does Steve finally ask to try on?

Language discovery

1 POLITE REQUESTS: ASKING TO DO SOMETHING YOURSELF

When asking to do something yourself, you use the pattern **kǒr** + VERB + **nòy**; you can add **dâi mái?** at the end of the request for additional politeness:

ขอดูหน่อย(ได้ไหม)   **kǒr doo nòy (dâi mái)?**
                      Can I have a look, please?

ขอลองดูหน่อย(ได้ไหม) **kǒr lorng doo nòy (dâi mái)?**
                      Can I try it on, please?

> **LANGUAGE TIP**
> Remember, you use **kǒr** when asking to do something yourself; you cannot use it when asking someone else to do something for you.

2 dâi

dâi has several different meanings, depending on its position in a sentence. It occurs most commonly after a verb, when it means, *can, able to*. The pattern, VERB + **dâi mái?** means *Can I/you/he/she, etc. …?* A *yes* answer to such a question is **dâi**; a *no* answer is **mâi dâi**.

(**kǒr doo nòy dâi mái?**)   (**dâi / mâi dâi.**)

ขอดูหน่อยได้ไหม   ได้/ไม่ได้
Could I have a look, please?   *Yes/No.*

Negative statements, such as *I can't walk*, follow the pattern, VERB + **mâi dâi**.

เดินไม่ได้   **dern mâi dâi.**   *I can't walk.*

ใส่ไม่ได้   **sài mâi dâi**   *I can't wear it./It doesn't fit.*

1 How would you say the following?
   a   I can't eat (it).
   b   I can't go.

3 COLOURS

sěe (colour) occurs before a specific colour word when describing the colour of something:

เสื้อสีแดง	sêu-a sěe dairng	a red shirt/top
รองเท้าสีน้ำตาล	rorng táo: sěe núm dtahn	brown shoes

The most common colour words are:

สีแดง	sěe dairng	red	สีน้ำตาล	sěe núm dtahn	brown
สีเขียว	sěe kěe-o	green	สีดำ	sěe dum	black
สีเหลือง	sěe lěu-ung	yellow	สีขาว	sěe kǎo:	white
สีน้ำเงิน	sěe núm ngern	blue			

4 NOUN + CLASSIFIER + née/nún/nóhn

In Unit 4 we saw how a classifier has to be used when using numbers with nouns, in phrases like **lôok sǒrng kon** (*two children*). A classifier is also used to link **née** (*this*) and **nún/nóhn** (*that*) with a noun; the pattern is NOUN + CLASSIFIER + **née/nún/nóhn**:

เสื้อตัวนั้นเท่าไหร่	sêu-a dtoo-a nún tâo-rài?
	How much is that shirt?
รองเท้าคู่นี้เก้าร้อยบาท	rorng táo: kôo née gâo: róy bàht
	This pair of shoes is 900 baht.

2 How would you say the following?

a   I like this top.
b   That top is very pretty.
c   This pair of shoes doesn't fit.
d   I don't like that pair of shoes.

5 HOW?

How? questions which ask about the manner in which something is done follow the pattern, VERB + **yung-ngai?** While **yung-ngai** is the normal pronunciation in spoken Thai, the word is spelled as if it were pronounced **yàhng-rai**.

เป็นอย่างไร	bpen yung-ngai?
	How is it? / How are things?

3 How would you ask the following?

a   How do you get there? (i.e. How do you go?).
b   How do you eat it?

Practice

1 How would you ask the following?

   a what the price of something is _____

   b to have a look at something _____

   c to try something on _____

   d to try size seven _____

2 Use the prompts to respond to the salesgirl's questions.

Salesgirl:	lorng doo mái ká?
You:	(say, Yes) _____
Salesgirl:	sài ber a-rai ká?
You:	(say, size 10) _____
Salesgirl:	bpen yung-ngai ká?
You:	(say, It's pretty. I like it very much) _____

 # Pronunciation

 06.05 Listen to the audio and repeat after the speaker.

ká?	dâi mái ká?	doo nòy dâi mái ká?	kŏr doo nòy dâi mái ká?
krúp?	dâi mái krúp?	ber sìp dâi mái krúp?	kŏr lorng ber sìp dâi mái krúp?

 # Reading, writing and pronunciation

LIVE SYLLABLES AND DEAD SYLLABLES

So far, we have seen how the class of the initial consonant – whether it is low, mid or high class – influences the tone of a word in Thai. All of the words that you have read so far have ended in either a vowel sound (**-ah, -or, -ai:, -ai, -ao:, -ee, -oo**) or a **-m**, **-n**, or **-ng** sound. These words are all called live syllables. Live syllables can be prolonged, on and on, for as long as you have the breath and inclination.

In this lesson we are going to see how to recognize tones in dead syllables. Dead syllables end in a **-p, -t, -k** sound or a short vowel; syllables ending in a short vowel are much less common than those ending in a **-p, -t, -k** sound.

Unlike live syllables, dead syllables cannot be prolonged. It is physically impossible; try it, and you will turn red in the face with the effort, while any trace of sound stubbornly refuses to make itself heard. When reading dead syllables, you need to know (a) the class of the initial consonant, (b) the length of the vowel – is it a long vowel or a short vowel? – and (c) whether the final letter is pronounced as **-p**, **-t**, or **-k**. This last point needs some further explanation. Thai, like all languages, has a limited set of sounds. The Thai sound system doesn't, for example, include final **-s**, **-b**, **-g** sounds, even though the letters representing these sounds can occur at the end of a word. Thais automatically recognize that words ending in these letters should be pronounced with a final **-t**, **-p** and **-k** sound respectively (you may notice that a Thai with limited command of English will transfer this strategy to English words, and may pronounce the word *bus*, for example, as *but*). The full list of consonants in the Appendix indicates how each is pronounced both at the beginning and end of a word.

DEAD SYLLABLES WITH LOW CLASS INITIAL CONSONANTS

If the initial consonant in a dead syllable is low class, the tone will be either high or falling. How do we know which? If the vowel is short, then the tone is high; if the vowel is long, the tone is falling. Study the following examples carefully; make sure that you can recognize each of the key elements in each word: (a) the class of the initial consonant, (b) the length of the vowel, (c) the final consonant sound. Once you can do this listen to the audio of this section.

 06.06

Low class initial consonant + short vowel + **p/t/k** sound = HIGH TONE:

รับ	ยิบ	วัด	นิด	ลุก	ยุค
rúp	yíp	wút	nít	lóok	yóok

Low class initial consonant + long vowel + **p/t/k** sound = FALLING TONE:

รีบ	ลูบ	ยอด	มีด	นอก	มาก
rêep	lôop	yôrt	mêet	nôrk	mâhk

Low class initial consonant + short vowel = HIGH TONE:

คะ	นะ	ยุ	มิ
ká	ná	lóo	mí

DEAD SYLLABLES WITH MID CLASS INITIAL CONSONANTS

Dead syllables that begin with a mid class consonant are always pronounced with a low tone, regardless of whether the vowel is long or short:

06.07

Mid class initial consonant + short/long vowel + **p/t/k** sound = LOW TONE:

กับ	จูบ	ติด	บาท	ดึก	จาก
gùp	**jòop**	**dtìt**	**bàht**	**dèuk**	**jàhk**

Mid class initial consonant + short vowel = LOW TONE:

ปะ	กะ	ดุ	ติ
bpà	**gà**	**dÒO**	**dtì**

DEAD SYLLABLES WITH INITIAL HIGH CLASS CONSONANTS

Dead syllables that begin with a high class consonant are always pronounced with a low tone, regardless of whether the vowel is long or short:

 06.08

High class initial consonant + short/long vowel + **p/t/k** sound = LOW TONE:

ขับ	สอบ	ผิด	ขาด	หัก	ถูก
kùp	**sòrp**	**pìt**	**kàht**	**hùk**	**tòok**

High class initial consonant + short vowel = LOW TONE:

สะใจ	ฉะ	ผุ	ผิ
sà jai	**chà**	**pÒO**	**pì**

SUMMARY OF TONE RULES

The tone rules you have just met are summarized as follows.

Initial consonant class	Live syllable	Dead Syllable	
		Short vowel	**Long vowel**
Low class	Mid tone	High tone	Falling tone
Mid class	Mid tone	Low tone	Low tone
High class	Rising tone	Low tone	Low tone

SILENT อ AT THE BEGINNING OF A WORD

In Unit 5 you met words that began with a silent ห. There are also four words which begin with a silent อ. These are all pronounced with a low tone. All four words are very common so it is worth copying them down and memorizing them at this stage.

อยู่	อย่า
yòo	**yàh**
to be situated at	*don't*

อย่าง	อยาก
yàhng	**yàhk**
like, kind	*to like to*

> **LANGUAGE TIP**
> Make a copy of this table – as you did for the tone rules table in Unit 5 – and keep it close at hand when reading Thai words until you have absorbed the rules. Take your time at this stage to make sure that you can apply the principles summarized in this table when reading words that don't have tone marks.

Test yourself

Listen to the audio and check your answers in the Answer Key.

1 **How would you ask the following?**
   a How much is this?
   b How much is this top?
   c How much is that pair of shoes?
   d Can I have a look, please?
   e Can I try it on please?

2 **How would you say the following?**
   a I don't like green.
   b The yellow top isn't pretty.
   c The white shoes don't fit.

3 **How would you translate the following?**
   a lorng doo mái?
   b sài ber a-rai?
   c bpen yung-ngai?
   d sài dâi mái?

4 **Which of these words are live syllables, and which ones are dead syllables?**
   a ตอบ
   b กัน
   c ติด
   d ถูก
   e จาก
   f ราว
   g ไป
   h สุด

5 **What tone should these words be pronounced with?**
   a สาม   sahm
   b บอก   bork
   c ผิด   pit
   d ปาก   bpahk
   e รัก   ruk
   f รอบ   rorp
   g นิด   nit
   h ลาบ   lahp

6 **Here are some words from the conversations. How would you read them and what do they mean?**
   a บาท
   b แปด
   c มาก
   d หก
   e ชอบ
   f สิบ

SELF CHECK	
I CAN...	
○	...ask the price of things.
○	...ask to look at or try on something.
○	...shop for items by colour.
○	...read 'dead' syllables.

Review unit 2

1 Fill in the missing question word in these exchanges:

a **Sue** mee pêe nórng _____ kon ká?
   Wanpen sŏrng kon kà

b **Waiter** sùng _____ krúp?
   Somjit yung kà

c **Steve** rorng tạo: kôo née _____ krúp?
   Salesgirl gâo: róy bàht kà

d **Sue** kŏr doo nòy _____?
   Vendor dâi krúp

2 Read the following conversation and answer the questions.

Somjit	mee pêe nórng gèe kon ká?
Sue	mee pêe chai: kon nèung pĕe săo: kon nèung kà
Somjit	ah-yÓO tâo-rài ká?
Sue	pêe chai: ah-yÓO săhm-sìp hâh
	pêe săo: ah-yÓO săhm-sìp
Somjit	dtàirng ngahn láir-o rĕu yung ká?
Sue	pêe chai: yung mâi dtàirng ngahn
	pêe săo: dtairng ngahn láir-o
	mee lôok sŏrng kon
Somjit	pêe chai: tum ngahn a-rai ká?
Sue	bpen ah-jahn kà

a How many brothers and sisters does Sue have?
b How old are they?
c Is her brother married?
d How many children does her sister have?
e What does her brother do?

3 How would you read the following words?

เป็น   ซอย   แพง   ใช่   ผม

ไม่   ได้   ที่   แล้ว   มาก

คะ   บาท   คน   ถูก   ก็

4 How would you read the following phrases?

a มีลูกสองคน   c ชอบสีแดงไหม

b ไม่มีพี่น้อง   d กินเผ็ดเป็นไหม

5 Fill in the gaps a, b and c in this tone mark table.

Initial consonant class	Live syllable	Dead syllable	
		Short vowel	Long vowel
Low class	Mid tone	b _____	c _____
Mid class	Mid tone	Low tone	Low tone
High class	a _____	Low tone	Low tone

7 bpai sÒO-wun-na-poom mái?

Will you go to Suvarnabhumi?

In this unit you will learn how to:
- *carry out taxi transactions.*
- *talk about your language proficiency.*
- *recognize more low class consonants and wrap-around vowels.*

CEFR: *(A1) Can give instructions to a taxi driver and engage in typical 'small talk' conversation.*

 ## Taxis

Taxis provide a convenient and relatively cheap alternative to public transport in Bangkok. They run on meters, so you don't have to worry about haggling over the price. The three basic phrases that you need for taking a taxi journey are, **bpai … mái?** (*Will you go to …?*), **jòrt têe-nôhn** (*Pull up over there*) and **tâo-rài?** (*How much?*) – all, of course, followed by the appropriate polite particle.

Many drivers rent their vehicles for a 12-hour shift; if a driver thinks he is running short of time, he may refuse to take a passenger rather than risk a stiff penalty for returning the vehicle late. Outside Bangkok, there are no meters, and you have to agree a price before getting into the vehicle.

Taxi drivers may be happy to engage in conversation, in which case you have an excellent opportunity to practise your Thai. Conversations often follow a predictable pattern, enquiring about why you can speak Thai and where you come from. The Practice section offers an example of how you may try to initiate a short conversation yourself.

 How would you ask a taxi driver to take you to the post office?

Vocabulary builder

07.01 Listen to the audio and repeat each word after the speaker. Try to imitate the speaker as closely as you can, and try to think about the tone that you are hearing as you listen.

TAKING A TAXI

สุวรรณภูมิ	sÒO-wun-na-poom	*Suvarnabhumi (airport)*
พูด	pôot	*to speak*
เก่ง	gèng	*to be good at*
อยู่	yòo	*to live*
นาน	nahn	*a long time*
ลง	long	*to get off/out*
ถนนสุขุมวิท	ta-nŏn sÒO-kŎOm-wít	*Sukhumvit Road*
ซอย	soi:	*soi; a small road branching off a main road; it may be identified by a name, a number, or both*
ไม่ … หรอก	mâi … ròrk	*not … (contradiction)*
อ่าน	àhn	*to read*
เขียน	kĕe-un	*to write*
ภาษา	pah-sǎh	*language*
นิดหน่อย	nít-nòy	*a little bit*
ไม่ค่อย …	mâi kôy …	*not very, hardly*
เข้า	kâo	*to enter*
สถานีรถไฟ	sa-tǎh-nee rót fai	*railway station*
หรือ	lĕr?	*Really? Eh?*
แพง	pairng	*expensive*
รถ	rót	*car, vehicle*
ติด	dtìt	*to be stuck*

NEW EXPRESSIONS

ไปสุวรรณภูมิไหม	bpai sÒO-wun-na-poom mái?	*Will you go to Suvarnabhumi?*
พูดไทยเก่ง	pôot tai gèng	*You speak Thai well.*
อยู่เมืองไทยนานไหม	yòo meu-ung tai nahn mái?	*Have you lived in Thailand long?*
ลงที่ไหน	long têe-nǎi?	*Where do you want to get out?*
อ่านเป็นนิดหน่อย	àhn bpen nít-nòy	*I can read a bit.*
เขียนไม่ค่อยได้	kěe-un mâi kôy dâi	*I can't really write.*
รถติดมาก	rót dtìt mâhk	*The traffic is very bad.*
จอดที่โน่น	jòrt têe-nôhn	*Pull up over there.*

Conversations

 07.02 *Steve wants to go to the airport.*

1 What compliment does the taxi driver pay Steve?

Steve	ไปสุวรรณภูมิไหมครับ	bpai sÒO-wun-na-poom mái krúp?
Taxi	ไปครับ	bpai krup
	คุณพูดไทยเก่ง	kOOn pôot tai gèng
	เป็นคนชาติอะไร	bpen kon châht a-rai?
Steve	เป็นคนอังกฤษครับ	bpen kon ung-grìt krúp
Taxi	อยู่เมืองไทยนานไหม	yòo meu-ung tai nahn mái?
Steve	ไม่นานครับ	mâi nahn krúp
Taxi	มีแฟนคนไทยไหม	mee fairn kon tai mái?
Steve	ไม่มีครับ	mâi mee krúp
Taxi	ลงที่ไหนครับ	long têe nǎi krúp?
Steve	ที่นี่ก็ได้ เท่าไหร่ครับ	têe-nêe gôr dâi tâo-rài krúp?
Taxi	สามร้อยสี่สิบบาทครับ	sǎhm róy sèe-sìp bàht krúp

2 **Read and listen to the conversation again and answer these questions.**

a Has Steve been in Thailand long?

b Does Steve have a Thai girlfriend?

c How would you translate Steve's answer, têe-nêe gôr dâi?

d How much is the fare?

 07.03 *Sue is going to visit a friend who lives in a soi off Sukhumwit Road.*

3 **Which soi does Sue want to go to?**

Sue	ไปถนนสุขุมวิท	bpai ta-nǒn sÒO-kǒOm-wít
	ซอยสิบเก้าไหมคะ	soi: sìp-gâo: mái ká?
Taxi	ไปครับ	bpai krúp
	คุณพูดไทยเก่งครับ	kOOn pôot tai gèng krúp
Sue	ไม่เก่งหรอกค่ะ	mâi gèng ròrk kà
Taxi	แล้วอ่านเขียน	láir-o àhn kěe-un
	ภาษาไทยเป็นไหม	pah-sǎh tai bpen mái?
Sue	อ่านเป็นนิดหน่อยค่ะ	àhn bpen nít-nòy kà.
	แต่เขียนไม่ค่อยได้	dtàir kěe-un mâi kôy dâi
Taxi	เข้าซอยไหมครับ	kâo soi: mái krúp?
Sue	เข้าค่ะ จอดที่โน่นค่ะ	kâo kà jòrt têe-nôhn kà
	ใกล้ๆ รถสีขาว เท่าไหร่คะ	glâi glâi rót sěe kǎo: tâo-rài ká?

4 **Read and listen to the conversation again and answer these questions.**

a How does Sue respond to the taxi driver's compliment?

b Can Sue read and write Thai?

c Does Sue want to go into the soi?

d Where does she tell the taxi driver to pull up?

74

07.04 *Steve wants to take a train back to Bangkok.*

5 How much is the fare to the station?

Steve	ไปสถานีรถไฟเท่าไหร่ครับ	bpai sa-tăh-nee rót fai tâo-rài krúp?
Taxi	สามร้อยบาทครับ	săhm róy bàht krúp
Steve	สามร้อยบาทหรือครับ	săhm róy bàht lĕr krúp?
	สองร้อยห้าสิบได้ไหม	sŏrng róy hâh sìp dâi mái?
Taxi	ไม่ได้ครับ	mâi dâi krúp
	สามร้อยไม่แพงหรอกครับ	săhm róy mâi pairng ròrk krúp
	รถติดมาก	rót dtìt mâhk

6 Read and listen to the conversation again and answer these questions.
   a What fare does Steve suggest?
   b What is the taxi driver's reaction?
   c What justification does the driver give?

 Language discovery

1 ROMANIZING THAI WORDS

As we have already noted in Unit 1, the spelling of Thai words in Roman letters can seriously mislead the non-Thai speaker. The name of Bangkok's airport is a striking example. Written **Suvarnabhumi**, it is pronounced something like **soo-wun-na-poom** with not the slightest trace of a **v, b** or an **i**. The word comes from Sanskrit (the language of classical India, from which Thai has borrowed much vocabulary) and has been Romanized according to the convention for Romanizing Sanskrit words.

2 COMPLIMENTS

Thais are always willing to compliment foreigners on their efforts to speak Thai. Even the most feeble of attempts is likely to elicit an approving **pôot tai gèng** (*You speak Thai well*). But don't assume that this is an objective evaluation of your linguistic competence. Mutual compliments are an important element of Thai social interaction, and Thais are simply being nice when they say this. Sometimes, as in the first Conversation, it is little more than a formulaic playing for time, while the person thinks up the next question; but if there is sufficient pause for you to respond, the appropriate response is a modest denial, **mâi gèng ròrk** (*No, not at all*), not a smile and a *thank you.*

3 mâi … ròrk

ròrk is an untranslatable particle. It occurs in the pattern **mâi** + VERB/ADJECTIVE + **ròrk** to contradict another person's stated opinion or assumption, or reassure someone that things are not as bad as they perhaps fear:

kOOn pôot tai gèng krúp

คุณพูดไทยเก่งครับ
You speak Thai well.

mâi gèng ròrk kà

ไม่เก่งหรอกค่ะ
No, not at all.

sǒo-ay mái?

สวยไหม
Is it pretty?

mâi sǒo-ay ròrk

ไม่สวยหรอก
No, not at all.

1 Use mâi … ròrk to reassure Steve:

a Steve   glai mái krúp?
  You   _____

b Steve   pairng mái krúp?
  You   _____

c Steve   pèt mái krúp?
  You   _____

4 mâi kôy + VERB

mâi kôy … (*not very much, hardly*) is a useful way of softening negative statements or responses, so that they don't sound too blunt. VERB + **mâi kôy dâi** means *I/you/he/she/they can hardly …*

เขียนภาษาไทยไม่ค่อยได้   **kěe-un pah-sǎh tai mâi kôy dâi**
                                           I can hardly write Thai.

2 How would you say the following?

a I can hardly speak Thai. _____

b It's not very tasty. _____

c I don't like it very much. _____

d It's not very far. _____

 Practice

1 How would you say the following?
   a Will you go to Suvarnabhumi (Airport) please?
   b How much will you charge to go to the railway station?
   c 300 baht, eh? How about 250?
   d Pull up here, please.

2 You are going to visit a friend who lives off Sukhumwit Soi 49. Use the prompts to help you negotiate with the taxi driver.

You	a	(Ask if he will go to Sukhumwit Soi 49)
Taxi		bpai krúp käo soi: mái krúp?
You	b	(Say *Yes ... pull up over there.*)
Taxi		têe näi ná krúp?
You	c	(Say *Here will do* and ask the price.)

3 Use the prompts to engage the taxi driver in conversation.

You	a	(Ask him if he Is from Bangkok.)
Taxi		mâi châi krúp bpen kon ee-sähn krúp
You	b	(Ask him what province he comes from.)
Taxi		jung-wùt na korn pa-nom krúp
You	c	(Ask him if he has lived in Bangkok for a long time.)
Taxi		nahn krúp
You	d	(Ask him if he likes living in Bangkok.)
Taxi		mâi kôy chôrp krúp grOOng-tâyp rót dtìt mâhk

4 A Thai is asking you about your knowledge of Thai. Use the prompts to help you respond. Don't forget your polite particles at the end of each sentence.

Thai		kOOn pôot tai gèng kà
You	a	(Say *No, not at all.*)
Thai		yòo meu-ung tai nahn mái?
You	b	(Say *No.*)
Thai		kěe-un pah-säh tai bpen mái?
You	c	(Say *I can hardly write, but I can read a bit.*)

Pronunciation

 07.05 Listen to the audio and repeat after the speaker, paying careful attention to the tones.

nít-nòy	bpen nít-nòy	àhn bpen nít-nòy
nít-nòy	dâi nít-nòy	pôot dâi nít-nòy
dâi	mâi kôy dâi	kĕe-un mâi kôy dâi
bpen	mâi kôy bpen	pôot mâi kôy bpen

Reading and writing

 CONSONANTS

 07.06 The new consonants in this lesson are all low class consonants. You'll notice that you have already learned low class consonants that produce, **k**, **t**, **p**, **y** and **n** sounds in Units 1 and 4.

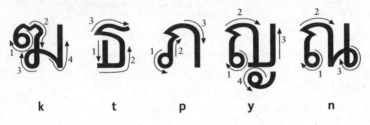

These new consonants are much less common than those you have already met, although they do occur in some very common words, such as the following:

ฆ่า	ภาษา	หญิง	ใหญ่	ญี่ปุ่น	คุณ
kâh	**pah-săh**	**yĭng**	**yài**	**yêe-bpÒOn**	**kOOn**
to kill	*language*	*female*	*big*	*Japan*	*you*

VOWELS

เา เีย เือ ◌ัว* เ◌ิ** -ะ

-ao	-ee-a	-eu-a	-oo-a	-er	-a
(short)	(long)	(long)	(long)	(long)	(short)

Most of the new vowel symbols are combinations of symbols you have already met which wrap around the consonant. The **-oo-a** and **-er** vowels have two written forms.

* When **-oo-a** is followed by a consonant, the top element of the vowel combination is omitted:

หัว	ตัว	บัว	*BUT*	สวย	ขวด	ด่วน
hŏo-a	**dtoo-a**	**boo-a**		**sŏo-ay**	**kòo-ut**	**dòo-un**

** When the **-er** vowel is not followed by a consonant, the top element of the vowel combination is omitted and 'zero consonant' added at the end.

เดิน	เปิด	เกิด	*BUT*	เจอ	เธอ
dern	**bpèrt**	**gèrt**		**jer**	**ter**

 07.07 **Practise reading these words.**

ภาค	ภาษา	ใหญ่	หญิง	คุณ	ฆ่า
pâhk	**pah-săh**	**yài**	**yĭng**	**kOOn**	**kâh**

เอา	เข้า	เท่าไหร่	ตัว	หัว	สวย
ao	**kâo**	**tâo-rài**	**dtoo-a**	**hŏo-a**	**sŏo-ay**

เสีย	เรียน	เขียน	เบื่อ	เหนือ	เดือน
sĕe-a	**ree-un**	**kĕe-un**	**bèu-a**	**nĕu-a**	**deu-un**

ช่วย	เกิน	เกิด	เดิน	เจอ	เธอ
chôo-ay	**gern**	**gèrt**	**dern**	**jer**	**ter**

ละ	จะ	คะ	ค่ะ	นะ	อะไร
lá	**ja**	**ká**	**kà**	**ná**	**a-rai**

Test yourself

07.08 **Listen to the audio and check your answers in the Answer Key.**

1 How would you say the following?
   a Will you go to the railway station?
   b How much will you charge to go to the airport?
   c Pull up over there.

2 How would you translate the following?
   a long têe năi krúp?
   b kâo soi: mái krúp?
   c săhm róy mâi pairng ròrk krúp rót dtìt mâhk

3 How would you say the following?
   a I can hardly speak Thai.
   b I can speak a little Thai.
   c I can read a little Thai.
   d I can't write Thai.

4 How would you translate the following sentences?
   a อยู่เมืองไทยนานไหม
   b ชอบอยู่เมืองไทยไหม
   c เขียนภาษาไทยไม่ค่อยได้

5 How would you read the following words?
   a คุณ you
   b สวย pretty
   c ภาษา language
   d ช่วย to help
   e เขียน to write
   f เดิน to walk
   g เข้า to enter
   h เท่าไหร่ how much?

6 Read this passage about an Englishman called Sam and then answer the questions (in English).

แซมเป็นคนภาคเหนือ เขาอยู่เมืองไทยนาน มีแฟนคนไทย แซมพูดภาษาไทยเก่ง แต่อ่านไม่ค่อยได้

LANGUAGE TIP
Notice the vowel used in writing – and consequently pronouncing – *'Sam'* in Thai.

a What part of England does he come from?
b Has he been in Thailand long?
c Does he have a Thai partner?
d Does he speak Thai?
e Can he read Thai?

SELF CHECK

I CAN...
...carry out taxi transactions.
...talk about your language proficiency.
...recognize more low class consonants and 'wrap-around' vowels.
...read a simple passage in Thai.

8 săo ah-tít ja bpai têe-o têe-năi?

Where are going this weekend?

In this unit you will learn how to:
▶ *say the days of the week.*
▶ *express opinions and preferences.*
▶ *talk about plans for the future and past experiences.*
▶ *read words that begin with two consonants.*

CEFR: *(A1) Can express simple opinions and preferences and ask and answer questions about past experiences.*

Leisure time

chai: ta-lay (*the seaside*) is a popular destination for those seeking to escape the noise, fumes, and congestion of Bangkok. Hua Hin and Pattaya (pronounced **pút-ta-yah**, not *pa-tai-ya*) have long been popular with Thais and foreigners alike for weekend breaks. As the tourist industry has expanded and communications improved, places further afield, such as Krabi (pronounced **gra-bpèe**, not *crabby* or *grabby*) and islands such as Koh (pronounced **gò'** not *co*). Samui and the one-time penal colony, Koh Tao have grown in popularity.

But for those who enjoy the sights, smells and sounds of a **dta-làht** (*market*) then the huge weekend market at **sŏo-un ja-dtÒO-jùk** (*Jatuchak Park*) in north Bangkok is not to be missed.

Vocabulary builder

08.01 **Listen to the audio and repeat each word after the speaker. Try to imitate the speaker as closely as you can, and try to think about the tone that you are hearing as you listen.**

LEISURE TIME

เสาร์อาทิตย์	săo ah-tít	*weekend*
จะ	ja	*future time marker*
เที่ยว	têe-o	*to visit, make a trip*
ชายทะเล	chai; ta-lay	*seaside*
หัวหิน	hŏo a hĭn	*Hua Hin*
เคย	ker-ee	*to have ever done something*
น่าเที่ยว	nâh têe-o	*worth visiting*
อาหารทะเล	ah-hăhn ta-lay	*sea food*
ที่นั่น	têe-nûn	*there*
ต่างจังหวัด	dtàhng jung-wùt	*outside Bangkok; upcountry*
กระบี่	gra-bpèe	*Krabi*
สนุก	sa nòOk	*fun; to be fun*
พัก	púk	*to stay*
ที่	têe	*at*
โรงแรม	rohng-rairm	*hotel*
ก็	gôr …	*er …, well …*
วันเสาร์	wun săo	*Saturday*
ตลาดจตุจักร	dta-làht ja-dtÒO-jùk	*Jatuchak Market*
คิด	kít	*to think*
ว่า	wâh	*to think, hold an opinion*
บีทีเอ็ส	bee tee es	*BTS (Bangkok Mass Transport System) Sky Train*
ดีกว่า	dee gwàh	*better*
ถูก	tòok	*cheap*

NEW EXPRESSIONS

เสาร์อาทิตย์จะไปเที่ยว ที่ไหน	săo ah-tít ja bpai têe-o têe-năi?	Where are you going at the weekend?
อ้อ หรือ	ôr lěr?	Oh, really?
เคยไปไหม	ker-ee bpai mái?	Have you ever been?
ไม่เคยไป	mâi ker-ee bpai	I've never been
สนุกไหม	sa-nÒÒk mái?	Was it fun?
คิดว่า ...	kít wâh ...	I think that ...
จะไปแท็กซี่	ja bpai táirk-sêe	I'll go by taxi

Conversations

 08.02 *Wanpen is asking Steve about his weekend plans.*

1 Where is Steve going?

Wanpen	เสาร์อาทิตย์คุณสตีฟ	săo ah-tít kOOn Sa-dteef
	จะไปเที่ยวที่ไหนคะ	ja bpai têe-o têe-năi ká?
Steve	จะไปเที่ยวชายทะเลครับ	ja bpai têe-o chai: ta-lay krúp
Wanpen	อ้อหรือคะ	ôr lěr ká?
	ที่ไหนคะ	têe-năi ká?
Steve	หัวหินครับ	hŏo-a hĭn krúp
Wanpen	เคยไปไหมคะ	ker-ee bpai mái ká?
Steve	ไม่เคยครับ	mâi ker-ee krúp
Wanpen	หัวหินน่าเที่ยวมากค่ะ	hŏo-a hĭn nâh têe-o mâhk kà
	อาหารทะเลที่นั่นอร๊อยอร่อย	ah-hăhn ta-lay têe-nûn a-róy a-ròy

2 Read and listen to the conversation again and answer these questions.

   a Why does Steve decide to go there?

   b Has he ever been there before?

   c Why does Wanpen think it is a good place to visit?

3   What province has Sue visited?

Somchai	คุณซูเคยไปเที่ยว	kOOn Sue ker-ee bpai têe-o
	ต่างจังหวัดไหมครับ	dtàhng jung-wùt mái krúp?
Sue	เคยค่ะ	ker-ee kà
	เคยไปกระบี่	ker-ee bpai gra-bpèe
Somchai	สนุกไหมครับ	sa-nÒOk mái krúp?
Sue	สนุกดีค่ะ	sa-nÒOk dee kà
Somchai	พักที่ไหนครับ	púk têe-nǎi krúp?
Sue	ที่โรงแรมค่ะ	têe rohng-rairm kà
Somchai	เป็นอย่างไรครับ	bpen yung-ngai krúp?
	ดีไหม	dee mái?
Sue	ก็ … ดีค่ะ แต่แพง	gôr … dee kà dtàir pairng

4   Read and listen to the conversation again and answer these questions.

   a Did Sue enjoy her trip?   **c** What did she think of it?
   b Where did she stay?

5   When is Sue going to Jatuchak Market?

Sue	วันเสาร์ฉันจะไป	wun sǎo chún ja bpai
	ตลาดจตุจักรค่ะ	dta-làht ja-dtÒO-Jùk ká
Wanpen	คุณซูเคยไปไหมคะ	kOOn Sue ker-ee bpai mái ká?
Sue	ไม่เคย	mâi ker-ee
Wanpen	จะไปอย่างไร	ja bpai yung-ngai?
Sue	ก็ … คิดว่าจะไปแท็กซี่ค่ะ	gôr … kít wâh ja bpai táirk-sêe kà
Wanpen	ฉันว่าไปบีทีเอ็สดีกว่าค่ะ	chún wâh bpai BTS dee gwàh kà
	ถูกกว่าไปแท็กซี่	tòok gwàh bpai táirk-sêe
	แล้วรถไม่ติด	láir-o rót mâi dtìt

6 Read and listen to the conversation again and answer these questions.

   a Has Sue ever been to Jatuchak Market?

   b How does she plan to get there?

   c What suggestion does Wanpen make?

   d What reasons does she give?

 Language discovery

 08.05

1 DAYS OF THE WEEK

วันจันทร์	**wun jun**	*Monday*
วันอังคาร	**wun ung-kahn**	*Tuesday*
วันพุธ	**wun pÓOt**	*Wednesday*
วันพฤหัส	**wun pa-réu-hùt**	*Thursday*
วันศุกร์	**wun sÒOk**	*Friday*
วันเสาร์	**wun săo**	*Saturday*
วันอาทิตย์	**wun ah-tít**	*Sunday*
เสาร์อาทิตย์	**săo ah-tít**	*weekend*

The word **wun** (*day*) usually prefaces the name of the day. When talking about the day on which something happens, Thai does not use a preposition corresponding to English *on*; and if it is clear from the context whether the speaker is talking about this Monday or last Monday, then time markers (such as **ja**) are frequently omitted.

วันจันทร์ไปทำงาน	**wun jun bpai tum ngahn**
	On Monday I'm going to work.
เขากลับมาวันเสาร์	**káo glùp mah wun săo**
	He's coming back on Saturday.

1 How would you say the following?

   a On Tuesday I'm going to the bank.

   b On Friday I'm not going to work.

   c At the weekend I'm going to Hua Hin.

2 TALKING ABOUT THE FUTURE: ja + VERB

The particle **ja** can be used immediately before a verb to indicate future time; but **ja** is frequently omitted when it is obvious, either from the context of the conversation, or the use of an expression of time (e.g. tomorrow, next week, etc.), that the speaker is referring to the future.

เสาร์อาทิตย์จะไปเที่ยวที่ไหน **săo ah-tít ja bpai têe-o têe-năi?**
Where are going at the weekend?

จะไปอย่างไร **ja bpai yung-ngai?**
How will you get there?

2 **Wanpen has told you she is planning a trip outside Bangkok. Using *ja*, how would you ask her:**
   a what province she will visit?
   b if she will go for a long time?
   c where she will stay?

3 ker-ee + VERB

The pattern **ker-ee** + VERB indicates that the action of the verb has occurred in the past:

เคยไปกระบี่ **ker-ee bpai gra-bpèe** *I've been to Krabi.*

The negative, **mâi ker-ee** + VERB, means *have never …*:

ไม่เคยไปหัวหิน **mâi ker-ee bpai hŏo-a hĭn**
I've never been to Hua Hin.

Have you ever …? questions follow the pattern, **ker-ee** + VERB + **mái?**
A yes answer is **ker-ee**; a no answer is **mâi ker-ee**:

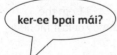

ker-ee bpai mái?   ker-ee/mâi ker-ee

เคยไปไหม   เคย/ไม่เคย
Have you ever been?   *Yes./No.*

3 **How would you say the following?**
   a Have you ever eaten Japanese food?
   b I've never been outside Bangkok.
   c I've been to/visited Krabi.

4 nâh + VERB

nâh occurs before a verb to form an adjective that conveys the sense *worth -ing*:

น่าเที่ยว	**nâh têe-o**	*worth visiting*	(**têe-o** to visit)
น่าอยู่	**nâh yòo**	*nice to live in*	(**yòo** to live)
น่ากิน	**nâh gin**	*tasty-looking*	(**gin** to eat)
น่ารัก	**nâh rúk**	*loveable, cute*	(**rúk** to love)

4 Can you guess the meaning of the following words?

a น่าสนใจ   nâh sŏn jai   (**sŏn jai** *to be interested in*)

b น่าเบื่อ   nâh bèu-a   (**bèu-a** *to be bored*)

c น่าเกลียด   nâh glèe-ut   (**glèe-ut** *to hate*)

d น่าเป็นห่วง   nâh bpen hòo-ung   (**bpen hòo-ung** *to be concerned*)

5 REDUPLICATION

In Unit 3 we stressed the fact that the repetition of an adjective usually makes the adjective less precise, rather than intensifying the meaning; we learned **glâi glâi** means *nearish* or *quite near*, not *very near*. But in Conversation 1 of this unit we find an example where reduplication is used to intensify the meaning, when Wanpen says, **ah-hăhn ta-lay têe nûn a-róy a-ròy** (*The seafood there is so tasty*). This kind of reduplication involves an exaggerated high tone on the first word which overrides the normal tone of the word. It is a common feature of female speech, but not used by male speakers.

6 gôr

The particle **gôr** serves a number of different functions. At the beginning of the sentence, it acts as a hesitation device, often showing some kind of reluctance, uncertainty, misgivings or unwillingness to cause offence on the part of the speaker:

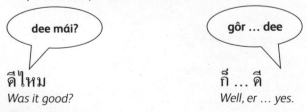

dee mái?

ดีไหม
Was it good?

gôr … dee

ก็ … ดี
Well, er … yes.

7 THINK THAT …

I think that … can be expressed using either **pŏm/chún kít wâh …** or **pŏm/chún wâh …** The pronoun **pŏm/chún** can be dropped before **kít**, but not before **wâh**.

คิดว่าจะไปแท็กซี่ **kít wâh ja bpai táirk-sêe**
I think I'll go by taxi.

ฉันว่าไปบีทีเอ็สดีกว่าค่ะ **chún wâh bpai BTS dee gwàh**
I think it's better to go by the BTS.

5 How would you say the following?
  a I think it was good fun.
  b I think I'll go to the seaside.
  c I think it's expensive.

8 COMPARISONS

The pattern ADJECTIVE + **gwàh** is used to express the idea *-er than, more … than*:

ไปบีทีเอ็สดีกว่า **bpai BTS dee gwàh**
It's better to go by BTS.

ถูกกว่าไปแท็กซี่ **tòok gwàh bpai táirk-sêe**
It's cheaper than going by taxi.

6 How would you say the following?
  a Thai food is tastier.
  b The post office is nearer.
  c Going outside Bangkok/upcountry is more fun.
  d The red top is prettier.

 Practice

1 You are asking a Thai friend about their plans for the weekend. Use the prompts to help you.

You	a	(Ask where your friend is going this weekend).
Thai		ja bpai têe-o gò' dtào kà
You	b	(Ask if she has ever been there.)
Thai		ker-ee kà
You	c	(Ask her if it was fun.)
Thai		sa-nÒOk mâhk kà

2 Your friend suggests a weekend trip to the seaside. Use the prompts to help you respond.

Thai		săo ah-tít bpai têe-o chai: ta-lay mái krúp?
You	a	(Ask where?)
Thai		pút-ta-yah gôr dâi hŏo-a hĭn gôr dâi
You	b	(Say you think it would better to go to Hua Hin.)
Thai		dee krúp hŏo-a hĭn nâh têe-o mâhk
You	c	(Ask where you will stay.)
Thai		têe rohng-rairm krúp
You	d	(Ask if the hotel is expensive.)
Thai		mâi pairng ròrk krúp

 Pronunciation

 08.06 Listen to the audio and repeat after the speaker, paying careful attention to the tones.

bpai táirk-sêe	ja bpai táirk-sêe	kít wâh ja bpai táirk-sêe
bpai BTS	ja bpai BTS	kít wâh ja bpai BTS
dee gwàh	bpai táirk-sêe dee gwàh	kít wâh bpai táirk-sêe dee gwàh
dee gwàh	bpai BTS dee gwàh	kít wâh bpai BTS dee gwàh

Reading and writing

WORDS BEGINNING WITH CONSONANT CLUSTERS

So far all the words that you've read have begun with either a single consonant or a vowel sound. Now we're going to look at words that begin with a consonant cluster (two consonant sounds) – words like **krúp**, **glùp**, **gwàh**, and so on. The tone of the word is always determined by the first consonant in the cluster:

ครับ   ขวา   ปลูก
krúp   **kwăh**   **bplòok**

In words that begin with a consonant cluster and are written with a tone mark, although the tone mark is written over the second consonant, the tone is actually determined by the initial consonant:

กว่า   ใกล้
gwàh*   **glâi***

* because mid class ก with **mái àyk** produces a low tone
** because mid class ก with **mái toh** produces a falling tone

All possible consonant clusters are listed as follows:

กร- gr-	คร- kr-	ขร- kr-	ตร- dtr	ปร- bpr-	พร- pr-
กล- gl-	คล- kl-	ขล- kl-		ปล- bpl-	พล- pl-
กว- gw-	คว- kw-	ขว- kw-			

Knowing which clusters can exist at the beginning of a word will help you avoid misreading words such as these:

สนุก   ตลาด   สบาย

Since these words begin with two consonants, they look very similar to those that begin with a consonant cluster. But from the consonant cluster table you can see that **sn-**, **dtl-** and **sb-** sounds do not exist in Thai. In order to read these words, a short, unwritten **-a** vowel has to be inserted between the first two letters; this first syllable is unstressed and pronounced with a mid tone.

So how about the tone in the second syllable? This is determined by the second consonant in the word (i.e. the first consonant of the second syllable) unless it is one of those consonants you learned in Unit 1 (น ม ง ร ล ย ว) or ณ; if the second consonant is a Unit 1 consonant or ณ, then it is the class of the first consonant which determines the tone:

 08.07

สนุก	ตลาด	สบาย	สภาพ	ขณะ	สนาม
sa-nÒOk	dta-làht	sa-bai:	sa-pâhp	ka-nà	sa-năhm

WORDS WITH NO VOWEL SYMBOLS (II)

You have already met words consisting of two consonants but no written vowel symbol, such as **kon** and **hòk**. Words consisting of three consonant symbols and no vowel symbols are much less common. These are two-syllable words, with an **-a** vowel in the first syllable and **-o** in the second:

ถนน	สงบ	ขนม	ตลก
ta-nǒn	sa-ngòp	ka-nǒm	dta-lòk

08.08 **Practise reading the following words**

กว่า	ขวา	ความ	ครับ	กรุง
gwàh	kwăh	kwahm	krúp	grOOng

ตรง	ใคร	ปรุง	ไกล	ปลา
dtrong	krai	bprOOng	glai	bplah

ถนน	ขนาด	สนุก	ตลก	สถาน
ta-nǒn	ka-nàht	sa-nÒOk	dta-lòk	sa-tăhn

สบาย	สยาม	ฉลาด	สภาพ	ขยัน
sa-bai:	sa-yăhm	cha-làht	sa-pâhp	ka-yŭn

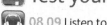

Test yourself

08.09 Listen to the audio and check your answers in the Answer Key.

1 **How would you say the following?**
   a Where did you stay?
   b How will you get there?
   c Was it fun?

2 **How would you translate the following?**
   a ah-hăhn ta-lay têe nûn a-róy a-ròy
   b chún wâh bpai BTS dee gwàh
   c tòok gwàh bpai táirk-sêe

3 **How would you answer these questions?**
   a săo ah-tít kOOn ja bpai têe-o têe-năi?
   b ker-ee bpai têe-o meu-ung tai mái?
   c ker-ee bpai têe-o dtàhng jung-wùt mái?

4 **How would you translate the following sentences?**
   a หัวหินน่าเที่ยวมาก
   b เคยไปไหม
   c คิดว่าจะไปแท็กซี่

5 **How would you read the following words?**
   a สนุก   fun   e กลับ   to return
   b กระบี่   Krabi   f สถานี   station
   c กว่า   -er than   g ประมาณ   about
   d ใกล้   near   h ถนน   road

6 **Write answers to the following questions.**
   a คุณเคยไปเที่ยวต่างจังหวัดไหม
   b คุณเคยไปเที่ยวหัวหินไหม
   c คุณเคยกินอาหารอีสานไหม

SELF CHECK

	I CAN...
○	...say the days of the week.
○	...express opinions and preferences.
○	...talk about plans for the future and past experiences.
○	...read words that begin with two consonants.

9 rót òrk gèe mohng?

What time does the bus leave?

In this lesson you will learn how to:
▶ *make travel arrangements.*
▶ *tell the time in full hours.*
▶ *read words written with shortened vowels.*

CEFR: *(A1) Can make simple enquiries about travel outside Bangkok; can understand simple time expressions.*

Travel

Travel outside Bangkok is cheap and convenient. The state-owned Mass Transport Organization operates a frequent, air-conditioned **rót too-a** (*tour bus, coach*) service to every province in the country from its Bangkok terminals, but you normally have to **jorng dtǒo-a** (*book a ticket*) in advance. Private companies, many operating from the Victory Monument area of Bangkok, also operate a shuttle **rót dtôo** (*minibus*) service to nearby provinces. A more leisurely and scenic way of travel is by **rót fai** (*train*) with the opportunity of booking a sleeper car for long journeys.

When booking tickets, you obviously need to be able to ask **rót òrk gèe mohng?** (*What time does the bus/train depart?*) – and then understand the answer, for telling the time in Thai is a little tricky: the only number in **sǒrng tÔOm** (*8 p.m.*), for example, is *two*, while the number **hâh** (*five*) occurs not only in *5 a.m.* and *5 p.m.*, but also *11 a.m.* and *11 p.m.*! But don't worry – all will be revealed in this unit.

 How would you ask where to book a ticket?

Vocabulary builder

09.01 **Listen to the audio and repeat each word after the speaker. Try to imitate the speaker as closely as you can, and try to think about the tone that you are hearing as you listen.**

TRAVEL

ออก	òrk	to leave, depart
สิบโมงเช้า	sìp mohng cháo:	10 a.m.
ซื้อ	séu:	to buy
ตั๋ว	dtǒo-a	ticket
จอง	jorng	to book
เชียงใหม่	chee-ung mài	Chiangmai
เมื่อไหร่	mêu-rài ?	when?
พรุ่งนี้	prÔOng née	tomorrow
เช้า	cháo:	morning
เต็ม	dtem	to be full
เย็น	yen	evening
สองทุ่ม	sǒrng tÔOm	8 p.m.
ที่	têe	seats

NEW EXPRESSIONS

ออกกี่โมง	òrk gèe mohng?	What time does it leave?
จะถึงกี่โมง	ja těung gèe mohng?	What time will it arrive?
ซื้อตั๋วที่ไหน	séu: dtǒo-a têe-nǎi?	Where do I buy a ticket?
อยากจะจองตั๋วไป …	yàhk ja jorng dtǒo-a bpai …	I'd like to book a ticket to …

Conversations

 09.02 *Sue is at a mini-bus terminal in Bangkok.*

1 Where does Sue want to go?

Sue	ขอโทษค่ะ	kŏr-tôht kà
	นี่รถไปหัวหินใช่ไหมคะ	nêe rót bpai hŏo-a hĭn châi mái ká?
Driver	ใช่ครับ	châi krúp
Sue	รถออกกี่โมงคะ	rót òrk gèe mohng ká?
Driver	สิบโมงเช้าครับ	sìp mohng cháo: krúp
Sue	ซื้อตั๋วที่ไหนคะ	séu: dtŏo-a têe-năi ká?
Driver	ที่โน่นครับ	têe-nôhn krúp
Sue	ขอบคุณค่ะ	kòrp-kOOn kà

2 Read and listen to the conversation again and answer these questions.
  a What time does the minibus leave?
  b Where should Sue buy a ticket?

 09.03 *Steve is at the bus terminal.*

3 Where does Steve want to go?

Steve	อยากจะจองตั๋ว	yàhk ja jorng dtŏo-a
	ไปเชียงใหม่ครับ	bpai chee-ung mài krúp
Clerk	จะไปเมื่อไหร่คะ	ja bpai mêu-rài ká?
Steve	พรุ่งนี้เช้าครับ	prÔOng née cháo: krúp.
Clerk	พรุ่งนี้เช้าเต็มแล้วค่ะ	prÔOng née cháo: dtem láir-o kà
	พรุ่งนี้เย็นได้ไหมคะ	prÔOng née yen dâi mái ká?
Steve	ก็...ได้ครับ	gôr … dâi krúp
	รถออกกี่โมงครับ	rót òrk gèe mohng krúp?
Clerk	สองทุ่มค่ะ	sŏrng tÔOm kà

4 Read and listen to the conversation again and answer these questions.

   a When does Steve want to travel?
   b Why can't he?
   c When can he travel?
   d What time does the bus leave?

 09.04 *Steve is still at the ticket kiosk.*

5 How many tickets does Steve want?

Clerk	พรุ่งนี้เย็นนะคะ	prôOng née yen ná ká
	เอากี่ที่คะ	ao gèe têe ká?
Steve	สองครับ	sŏrng krúp
Clerk	เก้าร้อยแปดสิบบาทค่ะ	gâo róy bpàirt sìp bàht kà
Steve	แล้วรถจะถึงกี่โมงครับ	láir-o rót ja tĕung gèe mohng krúp?
Clerk	ประมาณเจ็ดโมงเช้าค่ะ	bpra-mahn jèt mohng cháo: kà

6 Read and listen to the conversation again and answer these questions.

   a How much do the tickets cost?
   b What time will the bus reach Chiangmai?

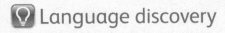

Language discovery

1 ASKING WHAT TIME SOMETHING HAPPENS

To ask what time something happens, you use the pattern VERB + **gèe mohng**?:

รถ(จะ)ออกกี่โมง **rót (ja) òrk gèe mohng?** *What time does the bus leave?*

The future time marker **ja** is optional and often omitted.

1 How would you ask someone the following?
  a What time are you going?
  b What time are you coming back (**glùp** *to return*)?
  c What time are you going to eat?

2 PARTS OF THE DAY

Before you can start to tell the time, you need to know the following words for parts of the day:

วัน	**wun**	*day*	บ่าย	**bài**	*afternoon*
คืน	**keu:n**	*night*	เย็น	**yen**	*evening*
เช้า	**cháo:**	*morning*			

3 TELLING THE TIME

Telling the time in Thai is complicated because the Thai equivalent of *o'clock* and the position of the number in relation to the *o'clock* word change according to the time of day. When telling hour times, you need to bear the following patterns in mind:

dtee + NUMBER	*1 a.m.–5 a.m.*
NUMBER + **mohng cháo:**	*6 a.m.–11 a.m.*
bài: + NUMBER + **mohng**	*1 p.m.–4 p.m.*
NUMBER + **mohng yen**	*5 p.m.–6 p.m.*
NUMBER + **tÔOm**	*7 p.m.–11 p.m.*

Here are the hours in full. Notice that the hours from 8 a.m. to 11 a.m. can be counted using numbers 8–11 + **mohng cháo:**, or in an alternative traditional way based on a division of the day into six hour periods, starting from 7 a.m., whereby 8 a.m. becomes *2 o'clock in the morning*, 9 a.m. *3 o'clock* … and so on. If a Thai suggests to you in English that you meet at 4 o'clock in the morning, you can possibly save yourself a long wait by checking that he really means 4 o'clock and not 10 o'clock. While it is easier to learn 8 a.m. as **bpàirt mohng cháo:**, 9 a.m. as **gâo mohng cháo:** and so on, you do at least need to be aware of the alternative way of expressing these times.

midnight	**têe-ung keu:n**	เที่ยงคืน
1 a.m.	**dtee nèung**	ตีหนึ่ง
2 a.m.	**dtee sǒrng**	ตีสอง
3 a.m.	**dtee sǎhm**	ตีสาม
4 a.m.	**dtee sèe**	ตีสี่
5 a.m.	**dtee hâh**	ตีห้า
6 a.m.	**hòk mohng cháo:**	หกโมงเช้า
7 a.m.	**jèt mohng cháo:**	เจ็ดโมงเช้า
8 a.m.	**bpàirt mohng cháo:**	แปดโมงเช้า
or	**sǒrng mohng cháo:**	สองโมงเช้า
9 a.m.	**gâo mohng cháo:**	เก้าโมงเช้า
or	**sǎhm mohng cháo:**	สามโมงเช้า
10 a.m.	**sìp mohng cháo:**	สิบโมงเช้า
or	**sèe mohng cháo:**	สี่โมงเช้า
11 a.m.	**sìp-èt mohng cháo:**	สิบเอ็ดโมงเช้า
or	**hâh mohng cháo:**	ห้าโมงเช้า
midday	**têe-ung wun**	เที่ยงวัน
1 p.m.	**bài mohng**	บ่ายโมง
2 p.m.	**bài sǒrng mohng**	บ่ายสองโมง
3 p.m.	**bài sǎhm mohng**	บ่ายสามโมง
4 p.m.	**bài sèe mohng**	บ่ายสี่โมง
5 p.m.	**hâh mohng yen**	ห้าโมงเย็น
6 p.m.	**hòk mohng yen**	หกโมงเย็น
7 p.m.	**tôOm nèung**	ทุ่มหนึ่ง
8 p.m.	**sǒrng tôOm**	สองทุ่ม
9 p.m.	**sǎhm tôOm**	สามทุ่ม
10 p.m.	**sèe tôOm**	สี่ทุ่ม
11 p.m.	**hâh tôOm**	ห้าทุ่ม

2 Match up the following times:

a sèe mohng cháo:

b sèe tÔOm

c bài sèe mohng

d dtee sèe

1	**04:00**
2	**16:00**
3	**10:00**
4	**22:00**

4 WHEN?

The question word **mêu-rài?** (*when?*) normally occurs at the end of a sentence. A time expression alone is often sufficient answer:

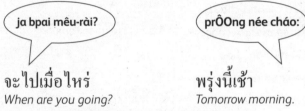

ja bpai mêu-rài?

prÔOng née cháo:

จะไปเมื่อไหร่
When are you going?

พรุ่งนี้เช้า
Tomorrow morning.

3 How would you ask the following?
a When will the bus leave?
b When will we arrive?
c When will he return?
d When will we eat?

Practice

1 How would you say the following?
  a Is this the bus for Hua Hin?
  b What time does the bus leave?
  c Where do I buy a ticket?
  d I'd like to book a ticket to Chiangmai.
  e What time does the bus arrive?

2 How would you translate the following?
  a ja bpai mêu-rài?
  b prÔOng née cháo: dtem láir-o
  c ao gèe têe?

3 You're booking tickets for a trip to the North. Use the prompts to help you.

You	**a**	(Say you'd like to book tickets to go to Lampang.)
Clerk		ja bpai mêu-rài ká?
You	**b**	(Say *Monday*.)
Clerk		wun jun dtem láir-o kà
		wun ung-kahn dâi mái ká?
You	**c**	(Say *yes* and ask what time the bus leaves.)
Clerk		săhm tÔOm kà

4 What time is it?
  a 05:00
  b 11:00
  c 17:00
  d 23:00

Pronunciation

 09.05 Listen to the audio and repeat after the speaker, paying careful attention to the tones.

ká?	gèe mohng ká?	ja òrk gèe mohng ká?	rót ja òrk gèe mohng ká?
ká?	gèe mohng ká?	ja tĕung gèe mohng ká?	rao ja tĕung gèe mohng ká?
ká?	mêu-rài ká?	ja gin mêu-rài ká?	rao ja gin mêu-rài ká?
ká?	mêu-rài ká?	ja glùp mêu-rài ká?	kOOn ja glùp mêu-rài ká?

 # Reading and writing

 CONSONANTS

 09.06 The consonants in this unit are rare; they don't occur in any of the words in this book and you don't need to worry about memorizing them at this stage. The class of each consonant is indicated beneath the letter.

ch

low

d

mid

dt

mid

t

high

t

low

t

low

l

low

h

VOWEL SHORTENER: –ะ

You have already met the vowel symbol —ะ as a short **-a** vowel in Unit 7.

The same symbol also has a completely different function in shortening the long vowels เ-, แ-, โ-, เ-อ and radically changing the pronunciation of เ-า:

เ-ะ	แ-ะ	โ-ะ	เ-อะ	เ-าะ
-e	-air	-o	-er	-o'

Practise reading these words:

เยะ	เตะ	เกะกะ	และ
yé	dtè	gè gà	láir

โต๊ะ	เยอะ	เยอะแยะ	เลอะเทอะ
dtó	yér	yér yáir	lér tér

เกาะ	เหมาะ	เพราะ	หัวเราะ
gò'	mò'	pró'	hŏo-a ró'

Test yourself

Listen to the audio and check your answers in the Answer Key.

1 How would you say the following?
 a What time does the Hua Hin bus leave?
 b The bus leaves at 8 p.m, right?
 c I'd like to book a ticket to Chiangmai tomorrow evening.
 d About what time does the bus reach Chiangmai?

2 How would you translate the following?
 a rót ja tĕung gèe mohng krúp?
 b séu: dtŏo-a têe-năi ká?
 c prÔOng née yen dâi mái ká?
 d bpra-mahn jèt mohng cháo:

3 How would you read the following words?

a	และ	and	e	เกาะ	island
b	โต๊ะ	table	f	เพราะ	because
c	เยอะ	a lot	g	หัวเราะ	to laugh
d	เยอะแยะ	a lot	h	เหมาะ	suitable

4 How would you read the following phrases?

 a รถออกกี่โมง

 b พรุ่งนี้เช้า

 c ซื้อตั๋วที่ไหน

 d จะไปเมื่อไหร่

 e รถจะถึงกี่โมง

 f พรุ่งนี้เย็น

 g อยากจะจองตั๋วไปเชียงใหม่

5 Read the following conversation and answer the questions in English.

Steve	จองตั๋วไปลำปางได้ที่ไหนครับ
Clerk	ที่นี่ค่ะ
	อยากจะไปเมื่อไหร่คะ
Steve	พรุ่งนี้ครับ
Clerk	พรุ่งนี้เย็นนะคะ
	รถออกหกโมงเย็น
	จะไปกี่คนคะ
Steve	สามคนครับ
Clerk	เก้าร้อยหกสิบบาทค่ะ
Steve	แล้วจะถึงกี่โมงครับ
Clerk	ประมาณตีสี่ตีห้าค่ะ

a Where does Steve want to go?
b When does he want to go?
c What time does the bus leave?
d How many tickets does Steve buy?
e How much do the tickets cost?
f What time will the bus reach its destination?

SELF CHECK

	I CAN...
◯	...make travel arrangements.
◯	...tell the time.
◯	...read words written with shortened vowels.

10 chôo-ay kĕe-un hâi nòy dâi mái?

Could you write it down for me, please?

In this unit you will learn how to:

▶ get Thais to repeat, translate, speak slowly and write things down.

▶ recognize some common diacritics and some irregularities in the writing system.

CEFR: *(A1) Can use simple requests to get a native speaker to translate or clarify the meaning of words, repeat phrases, speak slowly and write something down.*

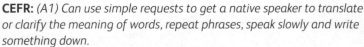

Getting help with your Thai

fung róo rêu-ung mái? (*Do you understand?*) is one of those questions you always dread. Like all good language learners, you've been confidently, or not so confidently, nodding your head and mmm-ing, by turns furrowing your brow and then smiling in a non-committal way. Suddenly the question brutally exposes the fact that you've been bluffing and haven't a clue what's going on, for people only ever ask you this when they already know the answer is no. How will you ever live with the shame of your ignorance and attempted deception being publicly exposed? One solution, of course, is to run away and never put yourself at risk again. Another, less radical option is to develop some coping strategies. **mâi róo rêu-ung** (*No, I don't understand*) you can admit, but follow it up immediately with something like **pah-săh ung-grìt bplair wâh a-rai?** (*What is it in English?*), which instantly removes the focus from you and puts the ball firmly back in your tormentor's court. **pah-săh tai rêe-uk wâh a-rai?** (*What's it called in Thai?*) is a useful way of demonstrating that, limited though your command of Thai may be, you have a serious interest in the language and a strong desire for self-improvement; and best of all – but only if you have done the script lessons in the book – is to ask, **chôo-ay kĕe-un hâi nòy dâi mái?** (*Could you write it down for me, please?*), which impresses everyone with the fact that you must be able to read Thai, and also conveniently masks the fact that you may have a bad ear for hearing the tone of a word in spoken Thai.

Vocabulary builder

10.01 **Listen to the audio and repeat each word after the speaker. Try to imitate the speaker as closely as you can, and try to think about the tone that you are hearing as you listen.**

เรียก	rêe-uk	*to be called*
อีกที	èek tee	*again*
ส้มตำ	sôm dtum	*papaya salad*
ช่วย…	chôo-ay …	*please …*
ให้	hâi	*for*
หยุด	yÒOt	*to stop*
ชั่วโมง	chôo-a mohng	*hour*
ครึ่ง	krêung	*half*
เวลา	way-lah	*time; at … (e.g. 4 p.m.)*
ฟัง	fung	*to listen*
รู้เรื่อง	róo rêu-ung	*to understand*
บอก	bòrk	*to say*
ทำไม	tum-mai	*why?*
ของกิน	kǒrng gin	*things to eat*
เข้าใจ	kâo jai	*to understand*
หนัง	nǔng	*film, movie*
ช้า	cháh	*slow*
หนังตลก	nǔng dta-lòk	*comedy*
แปล	bplair	*to translate*
ซี	see	*particle used to emphasize a positive response*

NEW EXPRESSIONS

ภาษาไทยเรียกว่าอะไร
pah-sŏh tai rêe-uk wâh a-rai?
What's it called in Thai?

เรียกว่า...
rêe-uk wâh …
It's called …

ช่วยพูดอีกทีได้ไหม
chôo-ay pôot èek tee dâi mái?
Could you repeat that, please?

ช่วยเขียนให้หน่อยได้ไหม
chôo-ay kĕe-un hâi nòy dâi mái?
Could you write it down for me, please?

ฟังรู้เรื่องไหม
fung róo rêu-ung mái?
Do you understand?

ไม่รู้เรื่อง
mâi róo rêu-ung
I don't understand

เขาบอกว่า...
káo bòrk wâh …
He said (that) …

เข้าห้องน้ำ
kâo hôrng náhm
to go to the toilet

ช่วยพูดช้า ๆ หน่อยได้ไหม
chôo-ay pôot cháh cháh nòy dâi mái?
Could you speak slowly, please?

ไม่เข้าใจคำว่า...
mâi kâo jai kum wâh …
I don't understand the word …

ภาษาอังกฤษแปลว่าอะไร
pah-săh ung-grìt bplair wâh a-rai?
What is it in English?

Conversations

 10.02 *Steve and Somjit are eating together.*

1 What is the name of the dish they are eating?

Steve	นี่ภาษาไทย	nêe pah-săh tai
	เรียกว่าอะไรครับ	rêe-uk wâh a-rai krúp?
Somjit	เรียกว่าส้มตำค่ะ	rêe-uk wâh sôm dtum kà
Steve	อะไรนะครับ	a-rai ná krúp?
	ช่วยพูดอีกทีได้ไหม	chôo-ay pôot èek tee dâi mái?
Somjit	เรียกว่าส้มตำค่ะ	rêe-uk wâh sôm dtum kà
Steve	ส้มตำใช่ไหม	sôm dtum châi mái?
Somjit	ใช่ค่ะ	châi kà
Steve	ช่วยเขียนให้หน่อย	chôo-ay kĕe-un hâi nòy
	ได้ไหมครับ	dâi mái krúp?

2 Read and listen to the conversation again and answer these questions:

  a How does Steve ask Somjit to repeat what she said?

  b What else does Steve want Somjit to do for him?

10.03 *Sue is on a bus travelling up-country when the bus pulls up and the driver makes an announcement.*

3 How long is the bus stopping for?

Driver	เราจะหยุดพักที่นี่	rao ja yÒOt púk têe-nêe
	ครึ่งชั่วโมงนะครับ	krêung chôo-a mohng ná krúp
	ช่วยกลับมาที่รถ	chôo-ay glùp mah têe rót
	เวลาสี่ทุ่มนะครับ	way-lah sèe tÔOm ná krúp
Thai	คุณฟังรู้เรื่องไหมคะ	kOOn fung róo rêu-ung mái ká?
Sue	ไม่รู้เรื่องค่ะ	mâi róo rêu-ung kà
Thai	เขาบอกว่า เราจะหยุดที่นี่	káo bòrk wâh rao ja yÒOt têe-nêe
	สามสิบนาทีนะคะ	sǎhm sìp nah-tee ná ká
Sue	หรือคะ จะหยุดทำไมคะ	lěr ká? ja yÒOt tum-mai ká?
Thai	ก็ ... หยุดพักค่ะ	gôr ... yÒOt púk kà
	อยากจะเข้าห้องน้ำก็เข้าได้	yàhk ja kâo hôrng náhm gôr kâo dâi
	อยากจะซื้อของกินก็ซื้อได้	yàhk ja séu: kǒrng gin gôr séu: dâi
	เข้าใจไหมคะ	kâo jai mái ká?
Sue	ก็ ... เข้าใจค่ะ	gôr ... kâo jai kà

4 Read and listen to the conversation again and answer these questions:
a What time do the passengers have to be back on the bus?
b How does the Thai explain the purpose of the stop?
c How well do you think Sue understands the explanation? Why?

5 Where does Wanpen want to take Sue?

Wanpen	พรุ่งนี้เย็นไปดูหนังไหม	prÔOng née yen bpai doo nŭng mái?
Sue	อะไรนะคะ	a-rai ná ká?
	ช่วยพูดช้า ๆ หน่อยได้ไหม	chôo-ay pôot cháh cháh nòy dâi mái?
Wanpen	พรุ่งนี้เย็น – ไป –	prÔOng née yen - bpai -
	ดูหนัง – ไหม	doo nŭng - mái?
Sue	หนังอะไรคะ	nŭng a-rai ká?
Wanpen	หนังตลกค่ะ	nŭng dta-lòk kâ
Sue	หนังยะไรนะคะ	nŭng a-rai ná ká?
Wanpen	หนังตลกค่ะ	nŭng dta-lòk kâ
Sue	ไม่เข้าใจคำว่า ตลกค่ะ	mâi kôo jai kum wâh dta-lòk kà
	ภาษาอังกฤษแปลว่าอะไร	pah-săh ung-grìt bplair wâh a-rai?
Wanpen	แปลว่า ฟันนี่ ค่ะ	bplair wâh 'fun-nêe' kà
	ไปไหม	bpai mái?
Sue	ไปซีคะ	bpai see ká

> **LANGUAGE TIP**
> Sue uses the particle **see** in the last line to indicate an enthusiastic *Oooh, yes*; notice that the particle **ká** when it follows **see** always has a high tone, even though it is not a question.

6 Read and listen to the conversation again and answer these questions:
  a When is the invitation for?
  b What word doesn't Sue understand?
  c Does she want to go?

Language discovery

1 ASKING SOMEONE TO DO SOMETHING

The pattern, **chôo-ay** + VERB is used when you want to ask someone to do something; although **chôo-ay** can mean *to help*, in requests it is simply a polite formula, like *please*. The particle **nòy** and **... dâi: mái?** (*could you ...?*) can also be added after the verb to make the request even more polite:

ช่วยพูดอีกทีได้ไหม
chôo-ay pôot èek tee dâi mái?
Could you say that again, please?

ช่วยกลับมาที่รถเวลาสี่ทุ่มนะครับ
chôo-ay glùp mah têe rót way-lah sèe tôOm ná krúp
Please come back to the bus at 10 p.m., OK?

ช่วยพูดช้า ๆ หน่อยได้ไหม
chôo-ay pôot cháh cháh nòy dâi mái?
Could you speak slowly, please?

The word **hâi** (*for*) is often added to **chôo-ay** requests to indicate who will benefit from the request, in the pattern **chôo-ay** + VERB + **hâi** (+ BENEFICIARY) + **nòy**:

In the first example the speaker himself is the beneficiary, so he would very probably omit the pronoun **pǒm**:

ช่วยเขียนให้(ผม)หน่อยได้ไหม
chôo-ay kěe-un hâi (pǒm) nòy dâi mái?
Could you write it down for me, please?

In the second example, a third party – *him* – is the beneficiary and therefore has to be specified:

ช่วยเขียนให้เขาหน่อยได้ไหม
chôo-ay kěe-un hâi káo nòy dâi mái?
Could you write it down for him, please?

1 How would you ask someone to:
   a translate something for you?
   b translate something for Steve?
   c buy something for you?
   d buy something for Steve?

2 UNDERSTAND

kâo jai and **róo rêu-ung** both mean *to understand*.

róo rêu-ung often occurs after the verb **fung** (*to listen*) to indicate the 'result' (i.e. understanding) that follows from listening. When Thais want to know whether a foreigner understands something said in Thai, they will ask **fung róo rêu-ung mái?**; if they want to check that someone – Thai or foreigner alike – has grasped the point they are making, they will ask **kâo jai mái?**

róo rêu-ung (not **fung**) is the verb that is used for *yes* answers and which is negated for *no* answers:

> fung róo
> rêu-ung mái?

> róo rêu-ung/
> mâi róo rêu-ung

ฟังรู้เรื่องไหม
Do you understand?

รู้เรื่อง/ไม่รู้เรื่อง
Yes./No.

Likewise, in negative statements, it is **róo rêu-ung** (not **fung**) which is negated:

ฟังไม่รู้เรื่อง   **fung mâi róo rêu-ung**   *I don't understand.*

3 wâh

In Unit 8 we met the word **wâh** after **kít** meaning *think that* and as a verb meaning *to think*. In this unit we see several more examples of **wâh**, after the verbs **rêe-uk** (*to be called*), **bplair** (*to translate*), **bòrk** (*to say*) and after the noun **kum** (*word*). Find these questions in the conversations, and see how **wâh** is used in some of the answers.

ภาษาไทยเรียกว่าอะไร   **pah-săh tai rêe-uk wâh a-rai?**
What's it called in Thai?

ภาษาอังกฤษแปลว่าอะไร   **pah-săh ung-grìt bplair wâh a-rai?**
What is it in English?

เขาบอกว่าเราจะหยุดที่นี่   **káo bòrk wâh rao ja yÒOt têe-nêe**
He said that we would stop here.

ไม่เข้าใจคำว่า ตลก   **mâi kâo jai kum wâh dta-lòk**
*I don't understand the word **dta-lòk**.*

2 How would you say the following?

  a In English it's called *comedy*.

  b What's *comedy* in Thai?

  c He said he wasn't going.

  d You said it didn't taste good, right?

In Unit 8 you met **gôr** at the beginning of a sentence where it acted as a hesitation device, giving the speaker time to think before giving a response.

In this unit we meet a different use of **gôr**, where it acts rather like *then* in the following sentences:

ไกลมาก(ฉัน)ก็ไม่ไป

glai mâhk (chún) gôr mâi bpai

If it's a long way, then I'm not going.

far – very – (I) – then – not – go

Note that **gôr** is followed by a verb; if a pronoun is used, it must come before **gôr**.

You may just be wondering where the Thai word for *if* has got to in this example. While there is a Thai word for *if* (**tâh**), it is very frequently omitted in normal spoken Thai, as you will notice in the second conversation:

อยากจะเข้าห้องน้ำก็เข้าได้

yàhk ja kâo hôrng náhm gôr kâo dâi

If you want to go to the toilet, then you can.

want to – go toilet – then – go – can

อยากจะซื้อของกินก็ซื้อได้

yàhk ja séu: kǒrng gin gôr séu: dâi

If you want to buy something to eat, then you can.

want to – buy – things to eat – then – buy – can

3 Leaving out *tâh*, how would you say the following?

   a If it's very spicy, then it isn't tasty.

   b If it's expensive, then I'm not buying it.

   c If you speak Thai, then I can't understand.

 Practice

1 How would you say the following?
   a Pardon? Could you repeat that please?
   b I don't understand. What is it in English?
   c Could you speak slowly, please?
   d What's this called in Thai?

2 How would you translate the following?
   a rao ja yÒOt púk têe nêe krêung chôo-a mohng ná
   b yàhk ja kâo hôrng náhm gôr kâo dâi
   c prÔOng née yen bpai doo nŭng mái?

3 You're having a problem understanding what a Thai friend is asking you. Use the prompts to help you.

Thai		ker-ee gin bpoo nŭng mái ká?
You	**a**	(Say *pardon?* and ask the person to repeat what they just said.)
Thai		ker-ee gin bpoo nŭng mái ká?
You	**b**	(Say you don't understand the words **bpoo nêung** and ask what they mean in English.)
Thai		bplair wâh *steamed crab* kà ker-ee gin mái ká?
You	**c**	(Say no.)

Pronunciation

 10.05 **Listen to the audio and repeat after the speaker, paying careful attention to the tones.**

cháh cháh nòy dâi mái?	chôo-ay pôot cháh cháh nòy dâi mái?
èek tee dâi mái?	chôo-ay pôot èek tee dâi mái?
kěe-un hâi nòy dâi mái?	chôo-ay kěe-un hâi nòy dâi mái?

 # Reading and writing

 You've now covered the main features of the Thai writing system. This unit looks at some further commonly used symbols and spelling irregularities you might encounter when reading an ordinary passage of Thai.

1 ฺ

When this symbol occurs above a consonant, that consonant is not pronounced. It occurs in words of foreign origin and reflects the spelling in the original language. Here are some examples from the course:

อาจารย์	เบอร์	อินเตอร์เน็ตคาเฟ่
ah-jahn	**ber**	**in-dter-net kah-fây**

ไปรษณีย์	เสาร์อาทิตย์	นักหนังสือพิมพ์
bprai-sa-nee	**săo ah-tít**	**núk núng-sěu pim**

Sometimes it is not only the consonant below the symbol which is not pronounced, but also the one immediately preceding it, as in the word for *Monday*:

วันจันทร์	**wun jun**	*Monday*
ศาสตร์	**sàht**	*science*

But occasionally, there is no symbol to indicate that the final consonant is not pronounced:

| ตลาดจตุจักร | **dta-làht ja-dtÒO-jùk** | *Jatuchak Market* |

2 - ๆ

This symbol **ๆ** indicates that the preceding word should be repeated:

ช้าๆ   **cháh cháh**   *slowly*

ใกล้ๆ   **glâi glâi**   *near*

3 - ฯ

You are most likely to meet this symbol in the word **grOOng-tâyp**, the Thai name for Bangkok. It really means *etc.* and is used to abbreviate the extremely long full name of the capital.

กรุงเทพฯ   **grOOng-tâyp**   *Bangkok*

4 r IN ung-grìt

The Thai spelling of **ung-grìt** (*English*) uses the extremely rare symbol **ฤ** to represent the **ri** sound:

อังกฤษ   **ung-grìt**   *English*

5 - รร -

When **- รร -** occurs between two consonants, it is pronounced **-u**:

สุวรรณภูมิ   **sÒO-wun-na-poom**   *Suvarnabhumi (airport)*

6 SILENT FINAL VOWEL

In some words of foreign origin, the final short vowel is silent:

ชาติ   **châht**   *nation*

สุวรรณภูมิ   **sÒO-wun-na-poom**   *Suvarnabhumi (airport)*

7 LINKER SYLLABLES

In a number of words a short unwritten **-a** vowel is inserted between two syllables to form a linker syllable. From the Thai spelling, **sÒO-wun-na-poom** looks as if it might be pronounced **sÒO-wun poom**, but the final **-n** in **wun** also acts as an initial **n** in the linker syllable **na**. Other examples include the words for *fruit* and *countryside*:

สุวรรณภูมิ	sÒO-wun-na-poom	Suvarnabhumi (airport)
ผลไม้	pǒn-la-mái	fruit
ชนบท	chon-na-bòt	countryside

8 MISMATCH BETWEEN PRONUNCIATION AND SPELLING

Generally speaking, there is a close match between the way a word is written in Thai and the way it is pronounced, so you have a very good chance of being able to pronounce unfamiliar words correctly when you see them written down. Inevitably, however, there are exceptions, typically where the tone or length of a vowel in normal spoken Thai differs from that suggested by the written form of the word.

Here are a few examples from earlier units:

ไหม	mái	high tone, not rising tone
ฉัน	chún	high tone, not rising tone
เขา	káo	high tone, not rising tone
… หรือยัง	…réu yung?	high tone on **réu**, not rising tone
จะ	ja	mid tone, not low tone
เก่ง	gèng	short vowel, not long
ข้างหลัง	kûng lǔng	short vowel on **kûng**, not long
เก้า	gâo:	long vowel, not short
รองเท้า	rorng táo:	long vowel on **táo:**, not short
น้ำ	náhm	long vowel, not short
หรือ	lěr?	vowel change from **-eu:**, consonant change from **r**
อย่างไร	yung-ngai?	short vowel and mid tone, not long vowel and low tone on first syllable; consonant change from **r** to **ng** on second syllable

10.06 Listen to the audio and check your answers in the Answer Key.

1 How would you say the following?
- **a** Could you speak slowly, please?
- **b** What is it in English?
- **c** Could you write it down for me, please?

2 How would you translate the following?
- **a** rao ja yÔOt púk têe nêe krêung chôo-a mohng ná krúp
- **b** chôo-ay glùp mah têe rót way-lah sèe tÔOm ná krúp
- **c** prÔOng née yen bpai doo nŭng mái?

3 How would you answer these questions?
- **a** 'nŭng dta-lòk' pah-săh ung-grìt rêe-uk wâh a-rai?
- **b** 'bpai doo nŭng' pah-săh ung-grìt bplair wâh a-rai?

4 How would you translate the following sentences?
- **a** เขาบอกว่า เราจะหยุดที่นี่สามสิบนาที
- **b** ช่วยพูดอีกทีได้ไหม
- **c** อยากจะเข้าห้องน้ำก็เข้าได้

5 How would you read the following words?
- **a** อังกฤษ
- **b** กรุงเทพฯ
- **c** เบอร์
- **d** ชาติ
- **e** ใกล้ๆ
- **f** อาจารย์
- **g** สุวรรณภูมิ
- **h** เสาร์อาทิตย์

6 Write answers to the following questions.
- **a** หนังตลก ภาษาอังกฤษแปลว่าอะไร
- **b** Papaya salad ภาษาไทยเรียกว่าอะไร

SELF CHECK

I CAN...
...get Thais to repeat, translate, speak slowly and write things down.
...recognize some common diacritics and some irregularities in the writing system.

1   **How would you say the following in Thai?**

   a   I've never been to Koh Tao.

   b   I think that it would be better to eat Thai food.

   c   He said that the bus leaves at about 8 p.m.

   d   What is **sa-nÒOk** in English?

   e   When is your (older) sister going to visit China?

   f   What time shall we eat?

   g   On Monday I'm going to the bank.

   h   Could you write that down for me, please?

2   **Read the following conversation and answer the questions.**

Wanpen	săo ah-tít ja bpai têe-o têe-năi ká?
Steve	ja bpai ra-yorng krúp
Wanpen	ra-yorng lěr? ker-ee bpai mái?
Steve	mâi ker-ee kOOn Wun-pen ker-ee bpai mái?
Wanpen	ker-ee kà
Steve	bpen yung-ngai?
Wanpen	sa-nÒOk dee kà bpai gèe wun?
Steve	sèe wun krúp
Wanpen	glùp wun ung-kahn châi mái?
Steve	châi krúp
Wanpen	ja bpai yung-ngai ká?
Steve	bpai rót too-a krúp
Wanpen	jorng dtŏo-a réu yung?
Steve	jorng láir-o
Wanpen	rót òrk gèe mohng ká?
Steve	sìp mohng cháo: krúp
Wanpen	ja púk têe-năi ká?
Steve	têe rohng-rairm krúp
Wanpen	pairng mái?
Steve	gôr … mâi kôy pairng krúp

a Where is Steve going at the weekend?

b Has he ever been there?

c Has Wanpen ever been there?

d How long is Steve going for?

e What day will he come back?

f How will he get there?

g Has he booked a ticket yet?

h What time does he depart?

i Where is he going to stay?

j Is it expensive?

3 How would you read the following words?

a	นะ	**d**	สนุก	**g**	เหนือ	**j**	สวย	**m** กรุงเทพฯ
b	คุณ	**e**	ใกล้ ๆ	**h**	เขียน	**k**	ถนน	**n** ภาษา
c	กว่า	**f**	ครับ	**i**	และ	**l**	อังกฤษ	**o** เท่าไหร่

4 How would you read the following phrases?

a รถติดมาก

b เข้าห้องน้ำ

c ไม่เคยไป

d ซื้อตั๋วที่ไหน

e ฟังรู้เรื่องไหม

f ช่วยพูดช้า ๆ หน่อยได้ไหม

g เขียนไม่ค่อยได้

h ภาษาอังกฤษแปลว่าอะไร

5 Read the following conversation and answer the questions.

Thai	คุณพูดไทยเก่ง เป็นคนชาติอะไรคะ
Foreigner	เป็นคนญี่ปุ่นค่ะ
Thai	อยู่เมืองไทยนานไหม
Foreigner	ไม่นานค่ะ
Thai	อ่านเขียนภาษาไทยเป็นไหม
Sue	อ่านเป็นนิดหน่อยค่ะ
แต่เขียนไม่ค่อยได้

a Is the Thai a male or female?

b Is the foreigner male or female?

c What nationality is the foreigner?

d Has the foreigner been in Thailand long?

e Can the foreigner read Thai?

f Can the foreigner write Thai?

Answer key

UNIT 1

Names and greetings

kOOn

Conversation 1

1 Wanpen **3** ah-jahn **4** kà **5** krúp

Language discovery 2

krúp, kà, ká

Conversation 2

1 mâi bpen rai kà **2** krúp **3** mâi bpen rai kà **4** In response to thanks.

Practice

1 a ah-jahn Sŏm-jìt **b** kOOn Sŏm-chai: **c** pŏm (I) is used by male speakers; chún (I) is used by female speakers **d** kà is used in statement; ká is used in questions. **2 a** kà; krúp **b** krúp; kà **c** ká; kà **d** krúp; kà **e** kà; krúp **3 a** sa-wùt dee krúp/ kà ah-jahn **b** bpai lá ná krúp/ká **c** kòrp-kOOn mâhk krúp/kà **d** kŏr-tôht krúp/kà **e** mâi bpen rai krúp/kà **4 a** sa-wùt dee krúp/kà **b** krúp/kà **c** mâi bpen rai krúp/kà or krúp/kà **d** mâi bpen rai krúp/kà

Test yourself

1 a sa-wùt dee krúp/kà **b** bpai lá ná krúp/ká **c** kòrp-kOOn krúp/kà **d** mâi bpen rai krúp/kà **e** kŏr-tôht krúp/kà **f** mâi bpen rai krúp/kà **2 a** sa-wùt dee krúp/kà **b** krúp/kà **c** mâi bpen rai krúp/kà or krúp/kà **d** mâi bpen rai krúp/ kà **3** Low class **4 a** mah **b** rum **c** yung **d** norn **e** yai: **f** lao:

UNIT 2

Bangkok and beyond

kon grOOng-tâyp

Vocabulary builder

What? normally occurs at the beginning of a question in English, while a-rai? normally occurs at the end of a question in Thai.

Conversations

1 Malika **2 a** kŏr-tôht/Excuse me **b** di-chún **c** kOOn Mah-li-gah châi mái krúp? **d** châi kà **3** No **4 a** kOOn Sa-dteef **b** British **c** ah-jahn **d** Lampang Province in the North

Language discovery

a Somjit uses **kOOn Sa-dteef** instead of just **kOOn** when talking to Steve, and Steve addresses Somjit as **ah-jahn** rather than **kOOn**.

b When Somjit says, **bpen kon pâhk nĕu-a kà**, she has deliberately omitted the word **di-chún** or **chún** (I).

Practice

1 a châi **b** châht; kon **c** jung-wùt **d** mâi châi **2 a** (kŏr-tôht) kOOn chêu: a-rai? **b** kOOn bpen kon châht a-rai? **c** kOOn bpen kon grOOng tâyp châi mái? **d** kOOn bpen kon pâhk dtâi: châi mái? **e** kOOn bpen kon jung-wùt a-rai? **3** (sample answers) **a** chêu: Sue kù **b** bpen kon ung-grìt kà **c** mâi châi kà **d** châi kà **4 a** 2 **b** 3 **c** 4 **d** 1

Go further

2 a Ireland **b** Russia **c** Belgium

Test yourself

1 a To show politeness **b** To confirm a statement/assumption **c** châi (yes), mâi châi (no) **d** grOOng-tâyp **e** pâhk (region) jung-wùt (province) **2 a** kŏr-tôht kOOn chêu: a-rai? **b** kŏr-tôht kOOn bpen kon grOOng-tâyp châi mái? **c** kŏr-tôht kOOn bpen kon jung-wùt a-rai? **d** káo bpen kon pâhk nĕu-a mâi châi kon grOOng-tâyp **3 a** mâi châi **b** mâi châi **4** Mid class **5 a** mee **b** bpai **c** gin **d** doo **e** nai **f** dee **6** lorn-dorn (London); lum-bpahng (Lampang)

UNIT 3

Conversations

1 An internet café **2 a** 5th floor **b** hâh **c** chún a-rai ná ká? **3** Yes **4 a** yòo têe- nôhn **b** He says No. **c** A post office **5** At the back, on the left **6 a** têe-nǎi?; the end **b** That it is on the left-hand side **c** tahng sái: châi mái krúp?

Language discovery

1 mee kà; mee krúp; mâi glai krúp **2** 5th floor **4** glâi glâi

Practice

1 a kŏr-tôht tăir-o née mee ta-na-kahn mái? **b** bprai-sa-nee yòo têe-năi?
c têe-nêe mee hôrng náhm mái? **d** glai mái? **2 a** 08913245 **b** 08673390
c 02317472 **3 a** glâi (falling tone) **b** glai (mid tone) **4** yòo glâi glâi a-rai ná?

Test yourself

1 a Is there a bank around here? **b** There's a bank around here, isn't
there? **2 a** mee; mâi mee **b** glai; mâi glai **c** châi; mâi châi **3 a** kŏr-tôht
tăir-o née mee hôrng náhm mái? **b** bprai-sa-nee yòo têe-năi? **c** têe-nêe
mee ta-na-kahn mái? **4 a** kŏrng **b** tŏOng **c** hăh **d** mŏr **e** lăi: **f** năi **5** To see
the doctor **6** Wanpen is going to visit Malika; Somchai is going too.

Review unit 1

1 a châi mái **b** a-rai **c** mái **d** têe-năi **2 a** male **b** female **c** post office **d** near
the bank **e** Chinese **f** Lin **g** Lek **h** Nakhorn Phanom **i** North-East **3 line 1** wun
kŏr doo mee năi **line 2** ngahn un bpai mŏr jahn **line 3** hăh dum nai gin
mohng **4 a** bpai lorn-dorn **b** bpai hăh mŏr **c** bpai doo nǔng

UNIT 4

Families

1 mee krúp/ kà **2** mâi mee krúp/ kà

Conversations

1 Yes **2 a** Two **b** Younger **c** Male **d** One is a journalist, the other is a
student. **3** Two **4 a** Middle **b** Eldest **c** Two **d** Boys **5** Yes **6 a** Older **b** Two
c A boy and a girl **d** The boy is 13, the girl 7

Practice

1 a mee/mâi mee **b** mee láir-o/yung **c** dtàirng láir-o/yung **2 a** mee **b** kon
c kon nèung **d** kon nèung **e** (láir-o) réu yung **f** yung **3 a** kŏr-tôht kOOn
dtàirng ngahn (láir-o) réu yung? **b** mee lôok (láir-o) réu yung? **c** lôok
ah-yÓO tâo-rài? **4 a** mee pêe chai: kon nèung, nórng săo: kon nèung
b mee nórng chai: sŏrng kon **c** mee pêe săo: sŏrng kon, nórng săo: kon
nèung **d** mâi mee pêe nórng

Test yourself

1 a mee pêe nórng mái? **b** mee pêe nórng gèe kon? **c** kOOn ah-yÓO
tâo-rài? **2 a** káo mee pêe nórng săhm kon **b** mee pêe săo: sŏrng kon,
nórng chai: kon nèung **c** mâi mee pêe nórng **3 a** dtàirng ngahn (láir-o)
réu yung? **b** mee lôok (láir-o) réu yung? **c** gin (láir-o) réu yung? **d** bpai
(láir-o) réu yung? **4 a** pŏm **b** káo **c** káo **d** káo **5 a** bpen **b** kon **c** tum
d pŏm **e** pairng **f** chai: **6 a** Chinese; rising tone **b** The North-East **c** Doctor

UNIT 5

Eating

a-ròy krúp/kà; pèt krúp/kà

Conversations

1 Yes **2 a** yung kà **b** Yes **c** Anything, he's not fussy **d** bpen mái? **e** bpen krúp **3** He's full. **4 a** a-ròy mâhk **b** ìm láir-o krúp **c** nórng ká! **d** chék bin dôo-ay **5** Fried rice **6 a** Shrimp fried rice **b** kà **c** Iced coffee **d** ao

Practice

1 a yung **b** mâi bpen **c** mâi yàhk **d** mâi châi **2 a** yàhk ja gin ah-hǎhn tai **b** kOOn Wun-pen yàhk ja gin ah-hǎhn pèt **c** kOOn Sue chôrp gin kâo: pùt **d** kOOn Sue yàhk ja gin kâo: pùt gÔOng **3 a** a-rai gôr dâi **b** têe-nǎi gôr dâi

Test yourself

1 a chôrp **b** bpen **c** châi **d** ìm láir-o **2 a** káo yàhk ja gin kâo: pùt **b** káo mâi yùhk ja gin ah-hǎhn pèt **c** kOOn Sue chôrp gin ah-hǎhn tai **d** kOOn Sue mâi chôrp gin ah-hǎhn jeen **3 a** What would you like? **b** Would you like some dessert? **c** Is it tasty? **d** Are you full? **4 a** sùng **b** ìm **c** mâi châi **d** dâi **e** láir-o **f** kâo: **5 a** Five **b** Older **c** Three **6 a** มี/ไม่มี **b** มี/ไม่มี **c** มี/ไม่มี **d** มี/ไม่มี **e** มี/ไม่มี

UNIT 6

Conversations

1 600 Baht **2 a** tâo-rài ná? **b** kǒr doo nòy dâi mái? **c** dâi krúp **d** 500 Baht **3** Red **4 a** 800 Baht **b** kǒr lorng doo nòy dâi mái? **c** She thinks it is very pretty. **5** No **6 a** 900 Baht **b** Size 9 **c** Size 10

Language discovery

1 a gin mâi dâi **b** bpai mâi dâi **2 a** chôrp sêu-a dtoo-a née **b** sêu-a dtoo-a nún sǒo-ay mâhk **c** rorng táo: kôo née sài mâi dâi **d** mâi chôrp rorng táo: kôo nún **3 a** bpai yung-ngai? **b** gin yung-ngai?

Practice

1 a nêe tâo-rài? **b** kǒr doo nòy dâi mái? **c** kǒr lorng doo nòy dâi mái? **d** kǒr lorng ber jèt dâi mái? **2 a** lorng **b** ber sìp **c** sǒo-ay chôrp mâhk

Test yourself

1 a nêe tâo-rài? **b** sêu-a dtoo-a née tâo-rài? **c** rorng táo: kôo nún tâo-rài? **d** kǒr doo nòy dâi mái? **e** kǒr lorng doo nòy dâi mái? **2 a** mâi chôrp sěe kěe-o **b** sêu-a sěe lěu-ung mâi sǒo-ay **c** rorng táo: sěe kǎo: sài mâi dâi **3 a** Do you want to try it on? **b** What size do you take? **c** How is it?

d Does it fit? **4 a** dead **b** live **c** dead **d** dead **e** dead **f** live **g** live **h** dead
5 a rising **b** low **c** low **d** low **e** high **f** falling **g** high **h** falling **6 a** bàht Baht
b bpàirt eight **c** mâhk very **d** hòk six **e** chôrp to like **f** sìp ten

Review unit 2

1 a gèe **b** réu yung **c** tâo-rài **d** dâi mái **2 a** two **b** 35 and 30 **c** no **d** two
e university lecturer **3 line 1** bpen soi: pairng châi pŏm **line 2** mâi dâi têe
láir-o mâhk **line 3** ká bàht kon tòok gôr **4 a** mee lôok sŏrng kon **b** mâi mee pêe
nórng **c** chôrp sĕe dairng mái? **d** gin pèt bpen mái? **5 a** rising **b** high **c** falling

UNIT 7

Discovery question

bpai bprai-sa-nee mái?

Conversations

1 You speak Thai well. **2 a** No **b** No **c** Here will do. **d** 340 baht **3** Soi 19
4 a She denies that she speaks Thai well. **b** She can read a bit but can't
really write. **c** Yes **d** Over there, by the white car. **5** 300 Baht **6 a** 250 Baht
b He says 'No'. **c** 300 Baht is not expensive and the traffic is bad.

Language discovery

1 a mâi glai ròrk **b** mâi pairng ròrk **c** mâi pèt ròrk **2 a** pôot pah-săh tai mâi
kôy dâi **b** mâi kôy a-ròy **c** mâi kôy chôrp **d** mâi kôy glai

Practice

1 a bpai sÒO-wun-na-poom mái? **b** bpai sa-tăh-nee rót fai tâo-rài?
c săhm róy bàht lĕr? sŏrng róy hâh sìp dâi mái? **d** jòrt têe-nôhn krúp/kà
2 a bpai ta-nŏn sÒO-kŎOm-wít soi: sìp-gâo: mái? **b** kâo krúp/kà jòrt
têe-nôhn **c** têe-nêe gôr dâi tâo-rài? **3 a** kŏr-tôht kOOn bpen kon grOOng-
tâyp châi mái? **b** jung-wùt a-rai? **c** yòo grOOng-tâyp nahn mái?
d chôrp yòo grOOng-tâyp nahn mái? **4 a** mâi gèng ròrk **b** mâi nahn
c mâi kôy bpen dtàir àhn bpen nít-nòy

Test yourself

1 a bpai sa-tăh-nee rót fai mái? **b** bpai sÒO-wun-na-poom tâo-rài?
c jòrt têe-nôhn krúp/kà **2 a** Where do you want to get out? **b** Do you want
to go into the soi? **c** 300 (Baht) isn't expensive. The traffic is very bad.
3 a pôot pah-săh tai mâi kôy dâi **b** pôot pah-săh tai dâi nít-nòy **c** àhn
pah-săh tai dâi nít-nòy **d** kĕe-un pah-săh tai mâi dâi **4 a** Have you been in
Thailand long? **b** Do you like living in Thailand? **c** I can't really write Thai.
5 a kOOn **b** sŏo-ay **c** pah-săh **d** chôo-ay **e** kĕe-un **f** dern **g** kâo **h** tâo-rài
6 a the North **b** Yes **c** Yes **d** Yes **e** Not very well.

UNIT 8

Discovery question

bpai dta-làht mái?

Conversations

1 Hua Hin **2 a** Because of the sea **b** No **c** Because of the seafood **3** Krabi
4 a Yes **b** At a hotel **c** It was OK, but expensive **5** Saturday **6 a** No
b By taxi **c** Go by BTS **d** It's cheaper and there are no traffic jams

Language discovery

1 a wun ung-kahn bpai ta-na-kahn **b** wun sÒOk mâi bpai tum ngahn
c săo ah-tít bpai hŏo-a hĭn **2 a** ja bpai têe-o jung-wùt a-rai? **b** ja bpai
nahn mái? **c** ja púk têe-năi? **3 a** ker-ee gin ah-hăhn yêe-bpÒOn mái?
b mâi ker-ee bpai têe-o dtăhng jung-wùt **c** ker-ee bpai têe-o gra bpèe
4 a Interesting; **b** boring; **c** detestable; **d** worrying **5 a** kít wâh sa-nÒOk
dee **b** kít wâh ja bpai têe-o chai: ta-lay **c** kít wâh pairng **6 a** ah-hăhn tai
a-ròy gwàh **b** bprai-sa-nee yòo glâi gwàh **c** bpai têe-o dtàhng jung-wùt
sa-nÒOk gwah **d** sêu-a săe dairng sŏo-uy gwàh

Practice

1 a săo ah-tít ja bpai têe-o têe-năi? **b** ker-ee bpai mái? **c** sa-nÒOk mái?
2 a têe-năi? **b** kít wâh bpai hŏo-a hĭn dee gwàh **c** ja púk têe-năi?
d pairng mái?

Test yourself

1 a kOOn púk têe-năi? **b** kOOn ja bpai yung-ngai? **c** sa-nÒOk mái?
2 a The sea food there is so delicious. **b** I think it's better to go by BTS.
c It's cheaper than going by taxi. **3 a** ja bpai … **b** ker-ee/mâi ker-ee
c ker-ee/mâi ker-ee **4 a** Hua Hin is really worth visiting. **b** Have you ever
been there? **c** I think I'll go by taxi. **5 a** sa-nÒOk **b** gra-bpèe **c** gwàh
d glâi **e** glùp **f** sa-tăh-nee **g** bpra-mahn **h** ta-nŏn **6 a** เคย / ไม่เคย
b เคย / ไม่เคย **c** เคย / ไม่เคย

UNIT 9

Discovery question

jorng dtŏo-a têe-năi?

Conversations

1 Hua Hin **2 a** 10 a.m. **b** Over there **3** Chiangmai **4 a** Tomorrow morning
b It's fully booked **c** Tomorrow evening **d** 8 p.m. **5** Two **6 a** 980 Baht
b About 7 a.m.

Language discovery

1 a kOOn ja bpai gèe mohng? **b** kOOn ja glùp mah gèe mohng? **c** kOOn ja gin gèe mohng? **2 a** 3 **b** 4 **c** 2 **d** 1 **3 a** rót ja òrk mêu-rài? **b** rao ja tĕung mêu-rài? **c** káo ja glùp mah mêu-rài? **d** rao ja gin mêu-rài?

Practice

1 a nêe rót bpai hŏo-a hĭn châi mái ká? **b** rót òrk gèe mohng? **c** séu: dtŏo-a têe-nǎi? **d** yàhk ja jorng dtŏo-a bpai chee-ung mài **e** rót ja tĕung gèe mohng? **2 a** When are you going? **b** Tomorrow morning is full. **c** How many seats do you want? **3 a** yàhk ja jorng dtŏo-a bpai lum-bpahng **b** wun jun **c** dâi rót òrk gèe mohng? **4 a** dtee hâh **b** sìp-èt mohng cháo:/ hâh mohng cháo: **c** hâh mohng yen **d** hâh tÔOm

Test yourself

1 a rót bpai hŏo-a hĭn òrk gèe mohng? **b** rót òrk way-lah sŏrng tÔOm châi mái? **c** yàhk ja jorng dtŏo-a bpai chee-ung mài prÔOng née yen **d** láir-o rót ja tĕung chee-ung mài gèe mohng? **2 a** What time does the bus arrive? **b** Where do I buy a ticket? **c** Is tomorrow evening OK? **d** About 7 a.m. **3 a** láir **b** dtó **c** yér **d** yér yáir **e** gò' **f** pró' **g** hŏo-a ró' **h** mò' **4 a** rót òrk gèe mohng? **b** prÔOng née cháo: **c** séu: dtŏo-a têe-nǎi? **d** ja bpai mêu-rài? **e** rót ja tĕung gèe mohng? **f** prÔOng née yen **g** yàhk ja jorng dtŏo-a bpai chee-ung mài **5 a** Lampang **b** Tomorrow **c** 6 p.m. **d** Three **e** 960 Baht **f** About 4 or 5 a.m.

UNIT 10

Discovery question

a-rai ná?

Conversations

1 sôm dtum **2 a** chôo-ay pôot èek tee dâi mái? **b** Write it down for him **3** half an hour **4 a** 10 p.m. **b** a chance to go to the toilet or get something to eat **c** Her hesitant answer suggests she might not have understood **5** to see a movie **6 a** tomorrow evening **b** dta-lòk **c** yes

Language discovery

1 a chôo-ay bplair hâi nòy dâi mái? **b** chôo-ay bplair hâi kOOn Steve nòy dâi mái? **c** chôo-ay séu: hâi nòy dâi mái? **d** chôo-ay séu: hâi kOOn Steve nòy dâi mái? **2 a** pah-săh ung-grìt bplair wâh/rêe-uk wâh comedy **b** comedy pah-săh tai bplair wâh/rêe-uk wâh a-rai? **c** káo bòrk wâh káo mâi bpai **d** kOOn bòrk wâh mâi a-ròy châi mái? **3 a** pèt mâhk gôr mâi a-ròy **b** pairng gôr mâi séu: **c** pôot pah-săh tai gôr fung mâi róo rêu-ung

Practice

1 a a-rai ná krúp/ká? chôo-ay pôot èek tee dâi mái? **b** mâi kâo jai pah-săh ung-grìt bplair wâh a-rai? **c** chôo-ay pôot cháh cháh nòy dâi mái? **d** nêe pah-săh tai rêe-uk wâh a-rai krúp/ká? **2 a** We'll stop here for half an hour, right? **b** If you want to go to the toilet, you can. **c** Tomorrow evening shall we go to see a movie? **3 a** a-rai ná krúp/ká? chôo-ay pôot èek tee dâi mái? **b** mâi kâo jai kum wâh bpoo nêung pah-săh ung-grìt bplair wâh a-rai? **c** mâi ker-ee

Test yourself

1 a chôo-ay pôot cháh cháh nòy dâi mái? **b** pah-săh ung-grìt bplair wâh a-rai? **c** chôo-ay kĕe-un hâi nòy dâi mái? **2 a** We'll stop here for a break for half an hour, OK? **b** Please return to the bus at 10 p.m., OK? **c** Shall we go to see a movie tomorrow evening? **3 a** What's nŭng dta-lòk called in English? **b** What does bpai doo nŭng mean in English? **4 a** He said we'd stop here for 30 minutes. **b** Could you repeat that, please? **c** If you want to go to the toilet, you can do so. **5 a** ung-grìt **b** grOOng-tâyp **c** ber **d** châht **e** glâi glâi **f** ah-jahn **g** sŎO-wun-na-poom **h** săo ah-tít **6 a** หนังตลก ภาษาอังกฤษแปลว่า comedy **b** Papaya salad ภาษาไทยเรียกว่าส้มตำ

Review unit 3

1 a mâi ker-ee bpai gò' dtào **b** kít wâh gin ah-hăhn tai dee gwàh **c** káo bòrk wâh rót òrk bpra-mahn sŏrng tÛOm **d** 'sa-nÒOk' pah-săh ung-grìt bplair wâh a-rai? **e** pêe săo: ja bpai têe-o bpra-tâyt jeen mêu-rài? **f** rao ja gin gèe mohng? **g** wun jun ja bpai ta-na-kahn **h** chôo-ay kĕe-un hâi nòy dâi mái **2 a** Rayong **b** No **c** Yes **d** 4 days **e** Tuesday **f** Tour bus **g** Yes **h** 10 a.m. **i** Hotel **j** Not very **3 line 1** ná sa-nÒOk nĕu-a săo-ay grOOng-tâyp **line 2** kOOn glâi glâi kĕe-un ta-nŏn pah-săh **line 3** gwàh krúp láir ung-grìt tâo-rài **4 a** rót dtìt mâhk **b** kâo hôrng náhm **c** mâi ker-ee bpai **d** séu: dtŏo-a têe-năi? **e** fung róo rêu-ung mái? **f** chôo-ay pôot cháh cháh nòy dâi mái? **g** kĕe-un mâi kôy dâi **h** pah-săh ung-grìt bplair wâh a-rai? **5 a** female **b** female **c** Japanese **d** No **e** Yes, a little **f** Not really

Thai–English glossary

อ่าน	àhn	*to read*
อะไร	a-rai	*what?*
อร่อย	a-ròy	*tasty*
อาหาร	ah-hăhn	*food*
อาหารทะเล	ah-hăhn ta-lay	*seafood*
อาจารย์	ah-jahn	*teacher, lecturer*
อายุ	ah-yÓO	*age*
เอา	ao	*to want*
บาท	bàht	*baht (unit of Thai currency)*
บีทีเอ็ส	BTS	*BTS; sky train*
เบอร์	ber	*size*
บอก	bòrk	*to say*
ไป	bpai	*to go*
เป็น	bpen	*to be*
… เป็นไหม	… bpen mái?	*can you …?*
แปล	bplair	*to translate*
ประมาณ	bpra-mahn	*about*
ไปรษณีย์	bprai-sa-nee	*post office*
ช้า	cháh	*slow*
ชาติ	châht	*nation*
ใช่	châi	*yes to a … châi mái? question*

ใช่ไหม	châi mái?	..., is that right?
ชายทะเล	chai: ta-lay	seaside
เช้า	cháo:	morning
ชื่อ	chêu:	first name; to have the first name ...
เชียงใหม่	chee-ung mài	Chiangmai
ชั่วโมง	chôo-a mohng	hour
ช่วย ...	chôo-ay ...	please ...
ชอบ	chôrp	to like
ฉัน	chún	I (female speaker)
ชั้น	chún	floor; storey
ได้	dâi	to be able; can
...ได้ไหม	... dâi mái?	Can I/you/he/she etc. ...?
ดี	dee	good
ดีกว่า	dee gwàh	better
เดิน	dern	to walk
ดิฉัน	di-chún	I (female, formal)
ดู	doo	to look at
ดูหนัง	doo nǔng	to see a movie
ต่างจังหวัด	dtàhng jung-wùt	outside Bangkok; up-country
แต่	dtàir	but
แต่งงาน	dtàirng ngahn	to get married
เต็ม	dtem	to be full
ติด	dtìt	to be stuck
ตัว	dtoo-a	classifier for shirts
ตั๋ว	dtǒo-a	ticket

อีก	èek	another; again
อีกที	èek tee	again
แฟน	fairn	boyfriend, girlfriend; partner; spouse
ฟัง	fung	to listen
กาแฟเย็น	gah-fair yen	iced coffee
กี่	gèe	how many?
เก่ง	gèng	to be good at
กิน	gin	to eat (informal)
ไกล	glai	far, to be far
ใกล้ ๆ	glâi glâi	near, to be near
ก็ ...	gôr ...	er ..., well, ...
กุ้ง	gÔOng	shrimp
กระบี่	gra-bpèe	Krabi
กรุงเทพฯ	grOOng-tâyp	Bangkok
ห้า	hâh	five
ให้	hâi	for
หัวหิน	hŏo-a hĭn	Hua Hin
ห้องน้ำ	hôrng náhm	toilet
อิ่ม	ìm	to be full up
อินเตอร์เนตคาเฟ่	in-dter-net kah-fây	internet café
จะ	ja	future time marker
เจ็ด	jèt	seven
จอง	jorng	to book
ค่ะ; คะ	kà/ kâh; ká	female polite particles
ขนม	ka-nŏm	dessert

เขา	káo	he, she, they
เข้า	kâo	to enter
เข้าใจ	kâo jai	to understand
ข้าว	kâo:	rice
ข้าวผัด	kâo: pùt	fried rice
เคย	ker-ee	to have ever done something
คิด	kít	to think
คน	kon	person
คู่	kôo	pair
ขวบ	kùu-up	years old (up to the age of about ten)
ขอ	kŏr	to ask for something; to ask to do something
ขอ ... หน่อย	kŏr ... nòy	Please could I ...?
ของกิน	kŏrng gin	things to eat
คุณ	kOOn	polite title: Mr/Mrs/Miss/Ms
คุณ	kOOn	you
ครึ่ง	krêung	half
ครับ	krúp	male polite particle
ข้างหลัง	kûng lŭng	behind, at the back
... แล้วหรือยัง	... láir-o réu yung?	... yet?
หรือ	lĕr?	Really? Eh?
ลง	long	to get off/out
ลูก	lôok	child
ลูกชาย	lôok chai:	son
ลูกสาว	lôok săo:	daughter

ลอง	lorng	*to try on/out something*
มาก	mâhk	*very, much*
ไม่	mâi	*not*
ไม่ค่อย …	mâi kôy …	*not very, hardly*
ไม่ … หรอก	mâi … ròrk	*not … (contradiction)*
ไหม	mái?	*question particle used in yes/ no questions*
มี	mee	*there is/are; to have*
เมื่อไหร่	mêu-rài ?	*when?*
น่าเที่ยว	nâh têe-o	*worth visiting*
นาที	nah-tee	*minute*
นาน	nahn	*a long time*
นี่	nêe	*this*
นี้	née	*this*
นิดหน่อย	nít-nòy	*a little bit*
น้องชาย	nórng chai:	*younger brother*
น้องสาว	nórng săo:	*younger sister*
นักหนังสือพิมพ์	núk núng-sẽu pim	*journalist*
นักศึกษา	núk sèuk-sǎh	*student*
นั้น	nún	*that*
หนัง	nǔng	*film, movie*
หนังตลก	nǔng dta-lòk	*comedy*
ออก	òrk	*to leave, depart*
ภาษา	pah-sǎh	*language*
แพง	pairng	*expensive*
พี่น้อง	pêe nórng	*brothers and sisters*

พี่สาว	pêe sǎo:	older sister
เผ็ด	pèt	spicy
ผม	pǒm	I (male speaker)
พูด	pôot	to speak
พรุ่งนี้	prÔOng née	tomorrow
พัก	púk	to stay
เรียก	rêe-uk	to be called
โรงแรม	rohng-rairm	hotel
รู้เรื่อง	róo rêu-ung	to understand
รองเท้า	rorng táo:	shoe(s)
รถ	rót	car, vehicle
ร้อย	róy	a hundred
หกร้อย	hòk róy	six hundred
สนุก	sa-nÒOk	fun; to be fun
สถานีรถไฟ	sa-tǎh-nee rót fai	railway station
สาม	sǎhm	three
ใส่	sài	to wear, put on
ซ้าย	sái:	on the left
เสาร์อาทิตย์	sǎo ah-tít	weekend
ซี	see	particle used to emphasize a positive response
สี	sěe	colour
สีแดง	sěe dairng	red
ซื้อ	séu:	to buy
เสื้อ	sêu-a	shirt, blouse, top
สิบสาม	sìp sǎhm	thirteen

ซอย	soi:	soi; lane
ส้มตำ	sôm dtum	papaya salad
สวย	sǒo-ay	pretty, beautiful
สวนจตุจักรค่ะ	sǒo-un ja-dtÒO-jùk	Jatuchak Park
สุวรรณภูมิ	sÒO-wun-na-poom	Suvarnabhumi (airport)
สอง	sǒrng	two
สั่ง	sùng	to order
ธนาคาร	ta-na-kahn	bank
ถนนสุขุมวิท	ta-nǒn sÒO-kǑOm-wít	Sukhumvit Road
ทาน	tahn	to eat (formal)
ไทย	tai	Thai
แถวนี้	tǎir-o née	around here, in this area
เท่าไหร่	tâo-rài?	how much?
ที่	têe	at
ที่	têe	seat
ที่ไหน	têe-nǎi?	where?
ที่นี่	têe-nêe	here
ที่โน่น	têe-nôhn	over there
ที่นั่น	têe-nûn	there
เที่ยว	têe-o	to visit, make a trip
ถูก	tòok	cheap
ทำไม	tum-mai?	why?
ทำงาน	tum ngahn	to work
อังกฤษ	ung-grìt	English
ว่า	wâh	to think, hold an opinion

เวลา	way-lah	*time; at … (e.g. 4 p.m.)*
อยากจะ …	yàhk ja …	*would like to …*
เย็น	yen	*evening*
อยู่	yòo	*to be situated at*
อยู่	yòo	*to live*
หยุด	yÒOt	*to stop*
อย่างไร	yung-ngai?	*how?*

The Thai alphabet

CONSONANTS

The Thai alphabet is normally described as having 44 consonants; even though two of these, **kǒr kòo-ut** and **kor kon**, fell out of use more than a century ago, they continue to appear on standard alphabet charts used in primary schools. The extremely rare letters **réu**, **reu:**, **léu** and **leu:** are not regarded as consonants, but appear after the letters **ror reu-a** and **lor ling** respectively in dictionaries.

The consonants are presented in Thai alphabetical order. Each consonant has a name, rather like 'a-for-apple, b-for-bat', which children learn in school. Knowing the names of letters may impress Thais, but it will not help you to read Thai. So if you have limited memory capacity, focus on learning the practical stuff – how each consonant is pronounced, both at the beginning and end of a word, and its class.

	name		initial	final	class
ก	gor gài	(*chicken*)	g	k	mid
ข	kǒr kài	(*egg*)	k	k	high
ฃ	kǒr kòo-ut	(*bottle*)	k	k	(obsolete)
ค	kor kwai:	(*buffalo*)	k	k	low
ฅ	kor kon	(*person*)	k	k	(obsolete)
ฆ	kor ra-kung	(*bell*)	k	k	low
ง	ngor ngoo	(*snake*)	ng	ng	low
จ	jor jahn	(*plate*)	j	t	mid
ฉ	chǒr chìng	(*small cymbals*)	ch	t	high
ช	chor cháhng	(*elephant*)	ch	t	low
ซ	sor sôh	(*chain*)	s	t	low
ฌ	chor (ga)cher	(*tree*)	ch	t	low
ญ	yor yǐng	(*girl*)	y	n	low
ฎ	dor chá-dah	(*theatrical crown*)	d	t	mid
ฏ	dtor bpa-dtùk	(*goad*)	t	t	mid
ฐ	tǒr tǎhn	(*base*)	th	t	high

ฑ	tor mon-toh	(*Montho, wife of the god Indra*)	th	t	low
ฒ	tor tâo	(*old man*)	th	t	low
ณ	nor nayn	(*novice*)	n	n	low
ด	dor dèk	(*child*)	d	t	mid
ต	dtor dtào	(*turtle*)	dt	t	mid
ถ	tŏr tŎOng	(*bag*)	t	t	high
ท	tor ta-hăhn	(*soldier*)	t	t	low
ธ	tor tong	(*flag*)	t	t	low
น	nor nŏo	(*mouse*)	n	n	low
บ	bor bai mái:	(*leaf*)	b	p	mid
ป	bpor bplah	(*fish*)	bp	p	mid
ผ	pŏr pêung	(*bee*)	p	p	high
ฝ	fŏr fáh	(*lid*)	f	p	high
พ	por pahn	(*tray*)	p	p	low
ฟ	for fun	(*tooth*)	f	p	low
ภ	por sŭm-pao	(*sailing ship*)	p	p	low
ม	mor máh	(*horse*)	m	m	low
ย	yor yúk	(*giant*)	y	depends on preceding vowel	low
ร	ror reu-a	(*boat*)	r	n	low
ฤ	réu	-	réu/rí/rer	-	
ฤๅ	reu:	-	reu:	-	
ล	lor ling	(*monkey*)	l	n	low
ฦ	léu	-	léu	-	
ฦๅ	leu:	-	leu:	-	
ว	wor wăirn	(*ring*)	w	depends on preceding vowel	low
ศ	sŏr săh-lah	(*pavilion*)	s	t	high
ษ	sŏr reu-sĕe	(*ascetic*)	s	t	high
ส	sŏr sĕu-a	(*tiger*)	s	t	high
ห	hŏr hèep	(*box*)	h	-	high
ฬ	lor jOO-lah	(*kite*)	l	n	low
อ	or àhng	(*bowl*)	-	-	mid
ฮ	hor nók hôok	(*owl*)	h	-	low

Vowels

-ัว-	-อ	-ะ	◌ั	-ัว	-า	-าย	-าว
-oo-u-	-or	-a	-u	-oo-a	-ah	-ai:	-ao:
◌ำ	◌ิ	-ือ	◌ี	◌ึ	◌ื	◌ุ	-ูย
-um	-i	-ew	-ee	-eu	-eu:	-OO	-oo-ee
◌ู	เ-	เ-ื	เ-ย	เ-อ	เ-อ	เ-อะ	เ-ะ
-oo	-ay	-e	-er-ee	-ay-o	-er (long)	-er (short)	-e
เ-า	เ-าะ	เ-ิ	เ-ีย	เ-ือ	แ-	แ-็	แ-ะ
-ao	-o'	-er (long)	-ee-a	-eu-a	-air (long)	-air (short)	-air (short)
โ-	ใ-	ไ-					
-oh	-ai	-ai					

Where the distinction between a long vowel and short vowel is not apparent from the Romanization, vowel length is indicated in brackets.

Thai numbers

0	ศูนย์	๐	sǒon	6	หก	๖	hòk	
1	หนึ่ง	๑	nèung	7	เจ็ด	๗	jèt	
2	สอง	๒	sǒrng	8	แปด	๘	bpàirt	
3	สาม	๓	sǎhm	9	เก้า	๙	gâo:	
4	สี่	๔	sèe	10	สิบ	๑๐	sìp	
5	ห้า	๕	hâh					

Numbers *12–19* are formed using **sìp** + unit; *eleven* is irregular, using **èt** instead of **nèung**:

11	สิบเอ็ด	๑๑	sìp-èt
12	สิบสอง	๑๒	sìp-sǒrng
13	สิบสาม	๑๓	sìp-sǎhm
14	สิบสี่	๑๔	sìp-sèe

Numbers *30–90* are formed using unit + **sìp**; *20* is irregular, using **yêe** instead of **sǒrng**.

20	ยี่สิบ	๒๐	yêe-sìp
30	สามสิบ	๓๐	sǎhm-sìp
40	สี่สิบ	๔๐	sèe-sìp
50	ห้าสิบ	๕๐	hâh-sìp
60	หกสิบ	๖๐	hòk-sìp
70	เจ็ดสิบ	๗๐	jèt-sìp
80	แปดสิบ	๘๐	bpàirt-sìp
90	เก้าสิบ	๙๐	gâo:-sìp

Numbers between *ten* and *100* are formed in a regular way with the exception of *21, 31, 41*, etc. where the word for *one* is **èt** and not **nèung**. In numbers *21–9*, **yêe-sìp** is often contracted to **yêep** in informal spoken Thai:

21	ยี่สิบเอ็ด	๒๑	yêe-sìp èt (yêep èt)
22	ยี่สิบสอง	๒๒	yêe-sìp sǒrng (yêep sǒrng)
23	ยี่สิบสาม	๒๓	yêe-sìp sǎhm (yêep sǎhm)
31	สามสิบเอ็ด	๓๑	sǎhm-sìp èt
32	สามสิบสอง	๓๒	sǎhm-sìp sǒrng
33	สามสิบสาม	๓๓	sǎhm-sìp sǎhm
41	สี่สิบเอ็ด	๔๑	sèe-sìp èt
42	สี่สิบสอง	๔๒	sèe-sìp sǒrng
51	ห้าสิบเอ็ด	๕๑	hâh-sìp èt

Numbers from *100* upwards are also formed regularly, but in addition to words for *thousand* and *million*, there are also specific words for *ten thousand* and *hundred thousand*:

100	(หนึ่ง) ร้อย	๑๐๐	(nèung) róy
101	(หนึ่ง) ร้อยเอ็ด	๑๐๑	(nèung) róy èt
102	(หนึ่ง) ร้อยสอง	๑๐๒	(nèung) róy sǒrng
1000	(หนึ่ง) พัน	๑๐๐๐	(nèung) pun
1002	(หนึ่ง) พัน(กับ)สอง	๑๐๐๒	(nèung) pun (gùp) sǒrng
1200	(หนึ่ง) พันสอง(ร้อย)	๑๒๐๐	(nèung) pun sǒrng (róy)
10,000	(หนึ่ง) หมื่น	๑๐๐๐๐	(nèung) mèu:n
100,000	(หนึ่ง) แสน	๑๐๐๐๐๐	(nèung) sǎirn
1,000,000	(หนึ่ง) ล้าน	๑๐๐๐๐๐๐	(nèung) láhn

"Global scale" of the Common European Framework of Reference for Languages: learning, teaching, assessment (CEFR)

Advanced	**CEFR LEVEL C2**	Can understand with ease virtually everything heard or read. Can summarise information from different spoken and written sources, reconstructing arguments and accounts in a coherent presentation. Can express him/herself spontaneously, very fluently and precisely, differentiating finer shades of meaning even in more complex situations.
	CEFR LEVEL C1	Can understand a wide range of demanding, longer texts, and recognise implicit meaning. Can express him/herself fluently and spontaneously without much obvious searching for expressions. Can use language flexibly and effectively for social, academic and professional purposes. Can produce clear, well-structured, detailed text on complex subjects, showing controlled use of organisational patterns, connectors and cohesive devices.
Intermediate	**CEFR LEVEL B2 (A Level)**	Can understand the main ideas of complex text on both concrete and abstract topics, including technical discussions in his/her field of specialisation. Can interact with a degree of fluency and spontaneity that makes regular interaction with native speakers quite possible without strain for either party. Can produce clear, detailed text on a wide range of subjects and explain a viewpoint on a topical issue giving the advantages and disadvantages of various options.
	CEFR LEVEL B1 (Higher GCSE)	Can understand the main points of clear standard input on familiar matters regularly encountered in work, school, leisure, etc. Can deal with most situations likely to arise whilst travelling in an area where the language is spoken. Can produce simple connected text on topics which are familiar or of personal interest. Can describe experiences and events, dreams, hopes and ambitions and briefly give reasons and explanations for opinions and plans.
Beginner	**CEFR LEVEL A2: (Foundation GCSE)**	Can understand sentences and frequently used expressions related to areas of most immediate relevance (e.g. very basic personal and family information, shopping, local geography, employment). Can communicate in simple and routine tasks requiring a simple and direct exchange of information on familiar and routine matters. Can describe in simple terms aspects of his/her background, immediate environment and matters in areas of immediate need.
	CEFR LEVEL A1	Can understand and use familiar everyday expressions and very basic phrases aimed at the satisfaction of needs of a concrete type. Can introduce him/herself and others and can ask and answer questions about personal details such as where he/she lives, people he/she knows and things he/she has. Can interact in a simple way provided the other person talks slowly and clearly and is prepared to help.